W9-DCH-106

2005 U.S. OPEN

JAMES BLAKE

Compiled and Edited
Eugene L. Scott

MARIA SHARAPOVA

JAMES BLAKE

WRITERS | Steve Flink
Lawrence Jeziak
Richard Pagliaro
Eugene L. Scott
Anne Smith

PHOTOGRAPHERS | Ron Angle
Michael Baz
Michael Cole
Melchior DiGiacomo
Ed Goldman
Cynthia Lum
Fred Mullane
Susan Mullane
Evan Pinkus
Art Seitz
Bob Straus
Angelo Tonelli
Paul Zimmer

ART DIRECTOR | Terry Egusa
MANAGING EDITOR | Andre Christopher
EDITOR | Kent Oswald

ISBN 0-9754777-3-0

15 Elm Place, Rye, New York 10580
Printed in China

CONTENTS

DEDICATION

TO THE PLAYERS... THE ONLY ONES WHO CAN KEEP UP WI

KIM CLIJSTERS

ROGER FEDERER

INTRODUCTION

The 2005 tournament was one of new heights being reached. Kim Clijsters earned a record payday — $2.2 million, with her U.S. Open prize money doubled because she won the lead-in, summer hardcourt U.S. Open Series. Roger Federer racked up his sixth straight Grand Slam final win — matching the 6-0 Grand Slam record last achieved by Tony Wilding, who took from 1906-13 to reach the same number of finals. Federer also became the first player since Don Budge in 1937-38 to win Wimbledon and the US. Open in the same season and back-to-back years.

What won't make the record books is the electricity in Arthur Ashe Stadium for the Andre Agassi – James Blake quarterfinal or the mystery of how the tic-laden performance of Mary Pierce enraptured new fans with every round of her march to the final. But all of this — money, records, electricity, mystery — as much as serves, forehands and backhands, is what created the magic of the 2005 U.S. Open.

On the following pages we remember and celebrate extraordinary people who excelled in a unique place and during an incredible time.

KIM CLIJSTERS

VANTAGE POINT

by Eugene L. Scott

Not surprisingly, the U.S. Open is often judged by weather not whether. By this measure, the Open had no equal. Clear days were followed by better days, followed by halcyon early-fall perfection. No humidity and no cancelled sessions brought huge smiles to players, fans and USTA bean counters who, for the first time in recent years, did not have to offer refunds, replacement tickets or gift cards for rain therapy. The latter three expenses are not trivial, and their absence, plus a series of five-set matches in Ashe Stadium, compounding food, beverage and merchandise sales, propelled the Open's gross revenues to nearly $210 million. A record for any annual sporting event in this country.

If brilliant sunshine and light seasonable breezes made for perfect playing conditions, what about the matches themselves? Brilliant also, but few breezes. Consider the tournament's top draw, Andre Agassi, battled in tiebreakers in six of his seven matches, three of which went five sets. Or that comebacker of this or any year, James Blake, did not have a straight set coast in his last three outings. Or that unseeded Robby Ginepri thrice thrashed over five sets during his gutsy semifinal run.

The women had no downhill trot either. Kim Clijsters over Venus Williams in three after Williams held an imposing set and service break lead was an upset to many, despite Kim being seeded 4th and Venus 10th, Williams, after all, had just won Wimbledon and had another four Grand Slam tournament singles titles in her portfolio. Kim had none. Next, Clijsters faced top seed Maria Sharapova and prevailed again in three sets. On the other side of the draw, No. 12 seed Mary Pierce confirmed her own credentials as the comeback player of the season, throttling three higher-ranked stars: Henin-Hardenne, Mauresmo and Dementieva, although the latter surely felt like doing some throttling herself after waiting an unacceptable 12 minutes for Pierce's injury time out. Her return from ranking obscurity is a testament to her discipline, hard work and competitive boil, which earned two Slam finals in three months. Her on-court mannerisms, if not manners, however, must be a mystery to fans and an annoyance to rivals. Pierce's flipping her ponytail, tugging on her eyelashes and sashaying about between points is not intentional gamesmanship, but is disruptive to opponents nonetheless. Her injury time out and toilet break during the hasty 65-minute final were diva moments indeed. Demonstrative fist rapping over her heart after she has won a tough point, game or match is sheer self-service. Her intended message cannot be what the gesture implies that, "I have heart; you don't."

Can you imagine Federer or Clijsters self-anointing themselves so?

The competition among the women, as expected, did not gain traction until the second week. In the fourth round, for example, only one of 16 players was unseeded. From the quarterfinals onward, on the other hand, tenacity and tension were pervasive. Contrast this with the battles rural from the start on the men's side, where 25 matches in the first round went to extra innings. By the fourth round, half the draw were unseeded. This loopy scenario for seeds had a single constant. Roger Federer. He started the Open as No. 1 seed and No. 1 in the world. He finished first too, with a gilded star next to his name that is certainly more asteroid than asterisk. His current caption must be The Untouchable. Losing but three sets in seven matches is an abridged tale. It tells nothing of his triumphing with grace, style and athletic facility, while not always playing his best, if this does not seem contradictory. Forget for an instant Federer's feline footwork during points. His movement back to the baseline after a point is not a walk. It is dressage without the unction.

If Federer's skills leading a hungry pack surrounding him is self-evident on court, the skills of the game's leadership off court is regrettably absent. To be fair, one has to explain the standard used here so that apples are not being compared to applesauce. Tennis, fortunately, has many talented entrepreneurs who have forged successful careers helping grow the game along the way. That is not what we're speaking of in this space. The model is Philippe Chatrier, the quintuple threat who was president of the French Tennis Federation for 10 years, president of the ITF for 10 years, president of the Men's International Pro Tennis Council in its formative years and savior of the French Open from mediocrity in the mid '70s. Not to mention singlehandedly bringing tennis back into the Olympics after a 60-year absence.

Chatrier's causes were not always popular, but popularity is never a leader's game plan. A true leader does what is right for the game regardless of objections from the peanut gallery.

For example, we have heard many players oppose Wimbledon's generous offer to move to a week later in the calendar ensuring more than 14 days between the French Open's clay and Wimbledon's grass. The Grand Slams, ATP and WTA should bless the change over some players' carping just because it is the

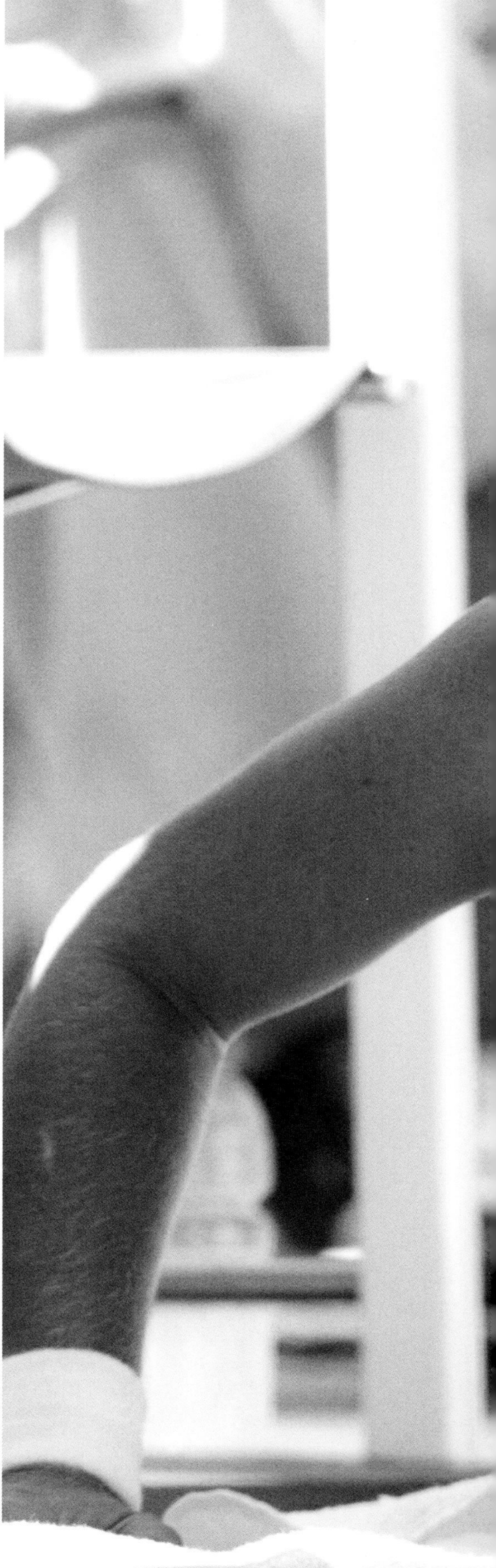

MARY PIERCE

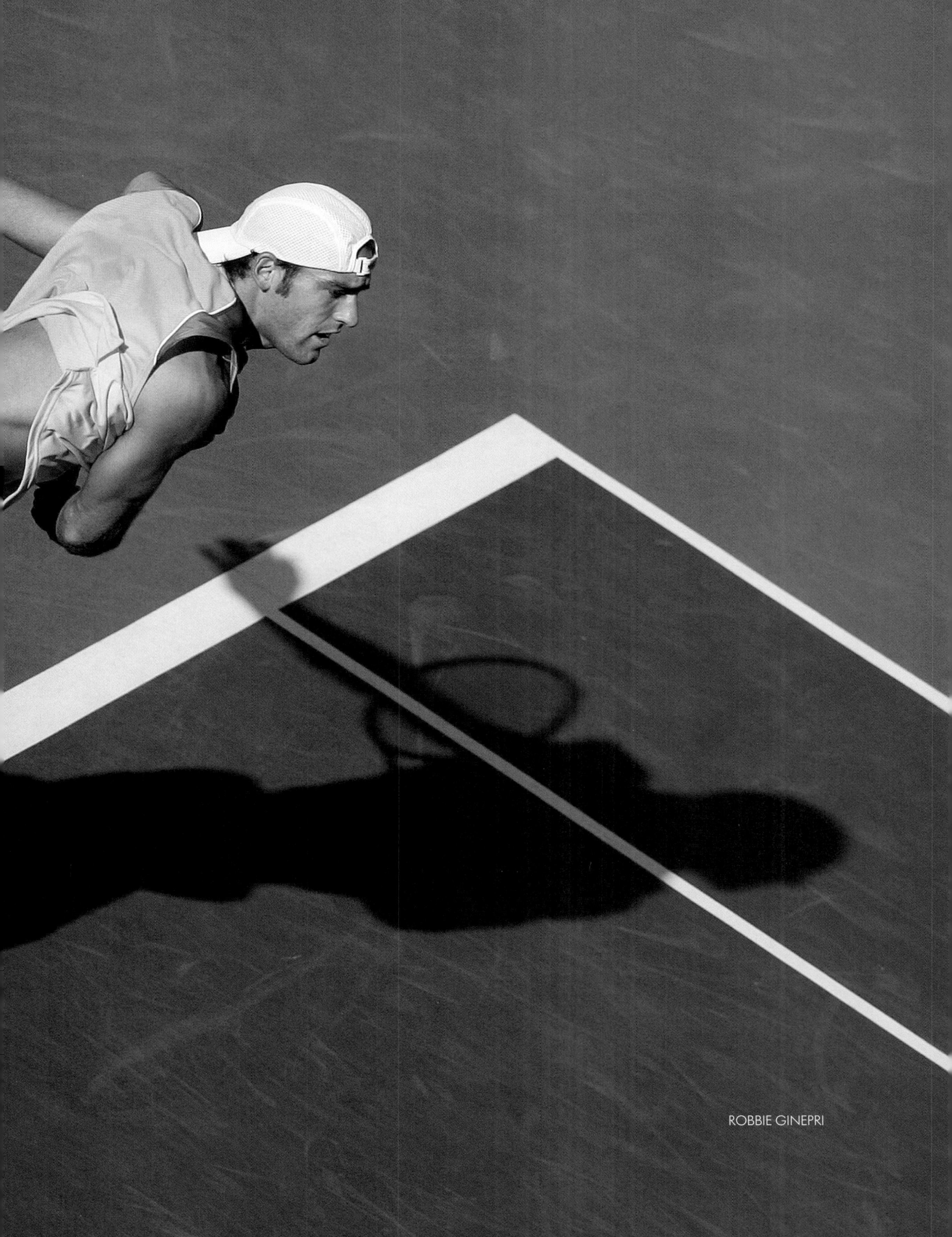

ROBBIE GINEPRI

BOB BRYAN (r) and MIKE BRYAN (l)

right thing to do. Period.

Similarly, the USTA tried mightily to find acceptable technology for electronic line calling in time for the 2005 U.S. Open. The systems examined ultimately were deemed not to be accurate enough to deploy this year. The level of accuracy sounded pretty good to this observer — something like a three percent tolerance level in one test. Do you think the decisions of line judges at Flushing Meadows come close to a three percent margin for mistake? A leader would have said, "In the interest of fans and players, this system is good enough. Let's go." Despite objections from a few very prominent players.

Leadership again was not in the building when the touring doubles players sued the ATP for marginalizing the tandem game to gradual extinction by 2008, when only singles players, plus two gratuitous wild cards, will be allowed in doubles draws. Not one representative from the ATP, USTA or ITF was present during a hastily assembled press conference during the Open. The irony is that everyone but doubles players, who have an obvious bias, should have appeared to fight for this cause. Doubles is as much a part of tennis as the net. Or, to put it another way, could you picture a court without doubles alleys? Chatrier wouldn't have allowed it. He wouldn't have punted either.

ANDRE AGASSI

SPECIAL DELIVERY

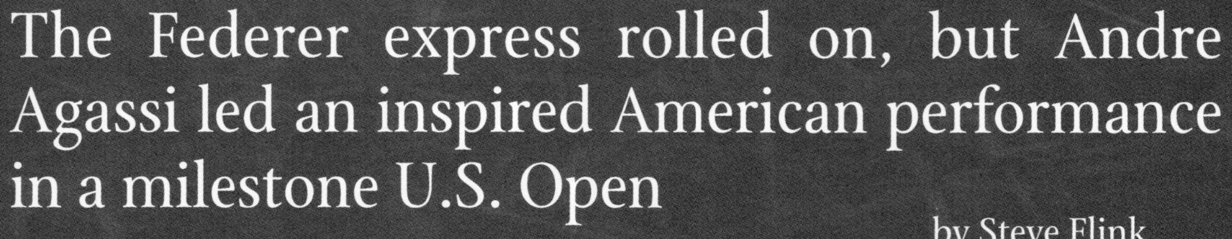

The Federer express rolled on, but Andre Agassi led an inspired American performance in a milestone U.S. Open

by Steve Flink

ANDRE AGASSI

LEXUS

It was not long after 7 p.m the U.S. Open's final Sunday in Arthur Ashe Stadium, and an almost ineffable Roger Federer was putting the finishing touches on a gripping final round triumph over none other than Andre Agassi. Federer was in full flow, serving at triple match point against the two-time former champion. The Swiss maestro sent one last second serve deep to Agassi's backhand, and the 35-year-old's return was long. Federer had eclipsed Agassi 6-3, 2-6, 7-6 (1), 6-1 for his second straight Open crown, his sixth major title victory without a loss, his 23rd final round triumph in a row and his 25th match win in a row since he lost to Rafael Nadal at the French Open. He had become the first man since Don Budge in 1937-38 to sweep the Wimbledon and U.S. Open singles titles two consecutive years. He had reaffirmed his greatness by besting Agassi in front of a Davis Cup-style crowd cheering the enduring American on unabashedly. It was Federer's finest hour at a major, and he enjoyed every minute of it.

"This was maybe the most special one for me," said the 24-year-old. "To play Andre in the final of the U.S. Open, [he is] still maybe one of the only living legends we have, next to Martina Navratilova on the women's side. To play him in this situation, him being toward the end of his career, me being on top of my game, and getting the chance to play him on such an occasion, ... I knew this was going to be very special."

It was for Agassi as well. He had come into the championship match having won three five set matches in a row over Xavier Malisse, James Blake and Robby Ginepri, but played his highest-quality tennis against Federer, who knocked off his old rival for the eighth time in a row after losing their first three encounters. One of those Agassi wins against Federer was a straight set demolition in 2001. Agassi came away this time with newfound respect for his conqueror.

"I just lost to a guy that's better. I mean, there's only so long you can deny it. He's the best I've ever played against," said Agassi, surprising even Federer by placing the Swiss genius above his former rival and 14-time major champion Pete Sampras in that category. "There's nowhere to go. There's nothing to do except hit fairways, hit greens and make putts. Every shot has that sort of urgency on it. ... There are other guys you play ... and there's a safety zone, a place to get to, something to focus on. Anything you do, he potentially has an answer for."

That was high praise from a man who pushed Federer close, but not quite to the brink in an absorbing battle. Agassi, of course, has pushed everyone at one time or another. This U.S. Open was his 20th in a row, tying him with Jimmy Connors for most consecutive U.S. Open appearances in the Open Era. By tournament's end, Agassi's 77 U.S. Open match wins trailed only Connors' 98, and at age 35, Agassi was the oldest man to play for a Grand Slam tournament title since 39-year-old Ken Rosewall lost to Connors in the 1974 U.S. Open championship match.

In this final, Federer surged to a 5-2, 0-40 lead in the opening set, but an obstinate Agassi held on before Federer went to 5-3, 40-0. Agassi refused to surrender again, saving four more set points. Federer finally held for the set, but his psyche had been shaken. Agassi took the second 6-2 behind two breaks and tenacious play on his own serve, then reached 4-2, 30-0 in the third. He was setting the agenda in the rallies, getting the meas-

ANDRE AGASSI

ure of Federer in many crosscourt forehand exchanges, and breaking down his foe's backhand. The American's forehand was breathtakingly penetrating, accurate and unerring.

Had Agassi held there and gone on to take a two-sets-to-one lead, he might have been able to claim the title. But Federer changed racquets just before the start of that seventh game, and with it, his game changed. He had the confidence again to go for his shots, to hit out on his backhand returns, to crack his forehand much closer to the lines. He broke back for 3-4 and from that point was virtually untouchable, winning 32 of 37 points on serve. Agassi managed to fend off four break points at 5-5, but in the tie-break, he lost seven points in a row after taking the first with a backhand drop shot winner. Federer had weathered the storm, and in the fourth set, swept 20 of 25 points on his way to 5-0 and soon closed out the match. In the last set and a half, the essential Federer emerged after a fortnight when he was often far below his highest standards.

Federer's semifinal showdown with No. 3 seed Lleyton Hewitt was a repeat of the 2004 final, but this time around the Swiss stylist did not soar to the heights he reached in his 6-0, 7-6 (3), 6-0 rout of the Australian a year ago. Federer was often listless during this year's 6-3, 7-6 (0), 4-6, 6-3 triumph over Hewitt, who broke a 16-set losing streak to Federer, but still lost for the ninth time in a row to the world No. 1. Federer secured the first set comfortably enough, then served with a 4-3, 30-0 edge in the second, only to blow a forehand volley from right on top of the net and went on to lose his serve. Hewitt pressed him hard from there. At 4-5, Federer fought off three set points; at 5-6, he saved two more. Every time, Federer struck gold, coming up with a brilliant backhand approach drop shot, three dazzling forehand winners and an unreturnable serve to reach the tie-break, where he sparkled for seven straight points.

But in the third set, Federer squandered five break points and played too passively. Hewitt took the initiative in rallies, served well on the big points and kept Federer at bay with his adroit shot selection. It was two sets to one. Federer's displeasure was apparent. With Hewitt serving at 2-3 in the fourth, the Australian was broken at love, donating two double faults, dealing himself an irrevocable blow. Federer was home free.

In addition to the coronation of Federer for the second year in a row, the big story for the men was not only Agassi's enduring excellence, but the excellence of American men overall. Two other Americans, Robby Ginepri and James Blake, made it to the semifinals and quarterfinals, respectively, against the odds. Taylor Dent, the third-highest ranked U.S. man entering the Open, fared well and was, indeed, impressive in extending Hewitt to five sets in the third round. Few believed Dent could endure such a contest after he retired from the Indianapolis final in exhaustion.

Even lesser-known American men, such as Brian Baker and Scoville Jenkins, had breakout performances, though they did not last to the second week of the tournament. Baker, the 2003 Roland Garros boys' singles runner-up who has received wild cards into the U.S. Open for the last three years, won his first Grand Slam tournament men's match, upsetting No. 9 seed Gaston Gaudio, the 2004 French Open champion, 7-6 (9), 6-2, 6-4, in the first round. Jenkins, in the spotlight last year as the U.S. junior champion unlucky enough to have to play defending champion Andy Roddick in the first round, returned to Flushing much improved, defeating George Bastl

ROBBIE GINEPRI

ROBBIE GINEPRI (l) AND ANDRE AGASSI (r)

in five sets for his first Grand Slam tournament match win and playing solidly in a 6-4, 7-5, 6-4 second round loss to No. 2 seed Rafael Nadal.

Roddick, on the other hand, the American expected to have the most realistic chance to take the title, fell in the first round, suffering a brutal blow to his pride.

Agassi's penultimate round meeting with Ginepri was by far the tightest skirmish yet between the two Americans. Ginepri had never taken a set in their three previous career collisions, including straight sets setbacks at the 2002 and 2004 U.S. Opens. But Ginepri is a decidedly more mature match player now. As his coach Francisco Montana said the day before Ginepri confronted Agassi, "Robby's shot tolerance has improved tenfold. If he has to keep nine, 10, 11 balls in during a rally, he will do that. He is patiently aggressive; whereas before, he pulled the trigger too soon. After he lost early at Wimbledon and his ranking dropped [from No. 74 to No. 103 in the ATP entry system], Robby put the blinders on and has played solid tennis ever since."

He had come into this contest with Agassi on a remarkable run of three consecutive five-set triumphs over No. 29 seed Tommy Haas, No. 13 Richard Gasquet and No. 8 Guillermo Coria. And the 22-year-old was not in awe of Agassi.

During the summer, Ginepri ousted Roddick on his way to winning Indianapolis and reached the semifinals of Cincinnati, losing a closely contested battle with Federer there. By the time he confronted Agassi in Ashe Stadium, Ginepri was a better player by far than he had ever been before. The first game of the fifth set was pivotal in this skirmish. Ginepri reached 15-40 on Agassi's serve. The Las Vegas native swung his first serve wide to the forehand, and Ginepri timidly chipped his return wide. Agassi followed with a thundering forehand into the clear off a high ball and held on. Thereafter, he swept 16 of 18 points on serve, including five aces, broke Ginepri for 4-2 and never looked back, coming through 6-4, 5-7, 6-3, 4-6, 6-3.

Despite that setback, Ginepri had enjoyed his strongest showing ever in a Grand Slam event. Losing to the redoubtable Agassi under the circumstances, Ginepri could not be too regretful. Perhaps the same can not be said for the immensely popular Blake, the 25-year-old African-American who has made such a stirring comeback after an astounding litany of woes set him back so severely a year ago.

Blake, who needed a wild card into the Open (or play qualifying) because his ranking was No. 107 when the cutoff came in July, had raised his stock considerably during the course of the U.S. Open Series. He was runner-up to Roddick in Washington and secured the singles title in New Haven. Blake had his devastatingly potent flat forehand going at full force again, his first serve was decidedly better and his backhand much more solid. Moreover, both before and during the Open, he displayed superb feel on the low volley.

After an impressive straight sets victory over No. 28 seed and former U.S. Open runner-up Greg Rusedski in the first round, Blake engineered a major upset when he toppled reigning French Open champion Nadal. All through their third round contest, Blake was driving his ground strokes with great depth, making Nadal scurry all over the court. The 19-year-old Spaniard — an impressive Masters Series hard court champion in Montreal where he upended Agassi in the final — was seldom able to show his propensity for moving from defense to offense with his incomparable foot speed.

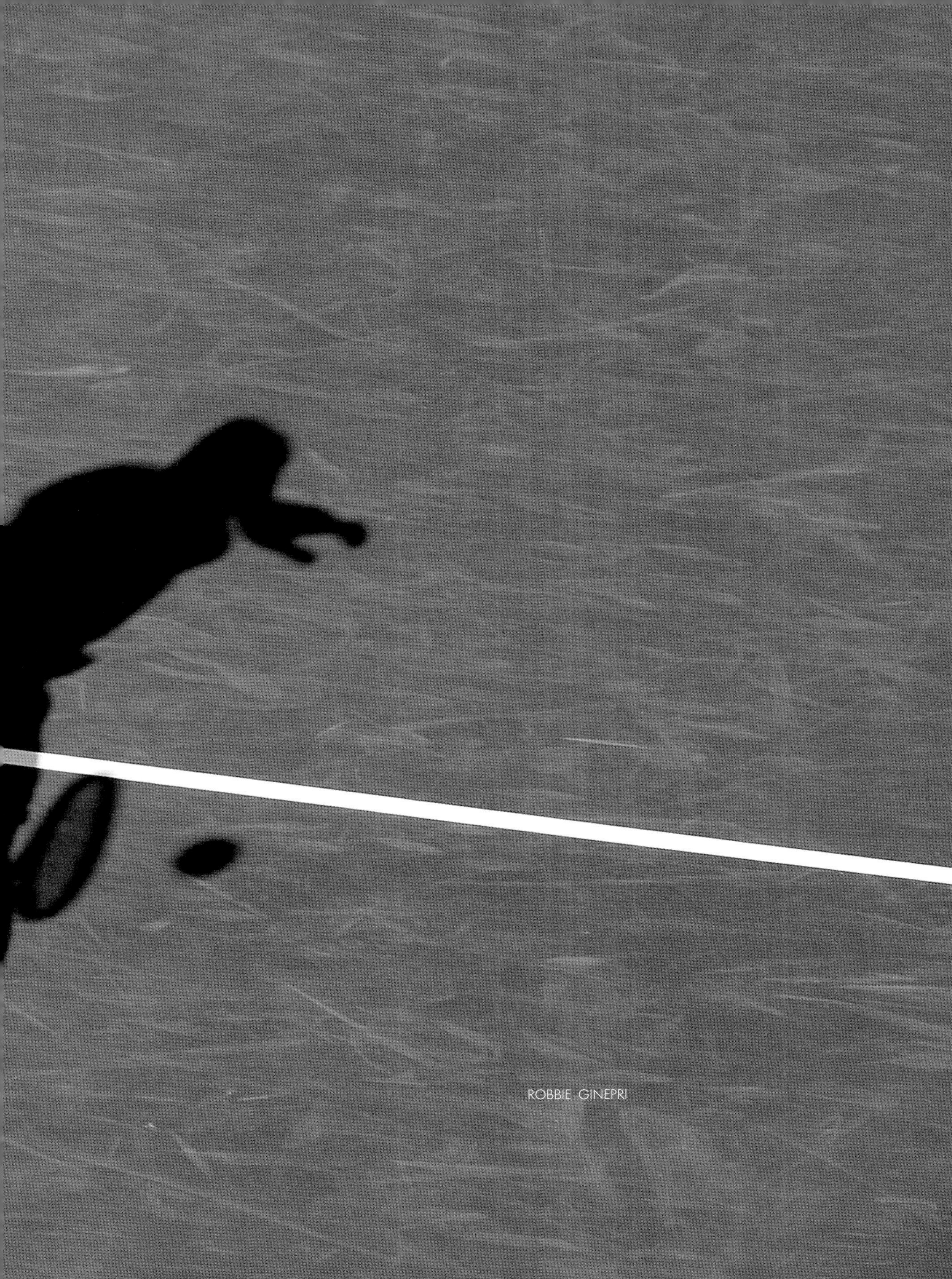
ROBBIE GINEPRI

LLEYTON HEWITT

Nadal was probably stifled by the overwhelmingly pro-Blake audience in Ashe Stadium. He was unusually subdued, his customary fist pumping seldom evident. Blake was moving forward at all the right times, winning 35 of 52 points when he approached the net against a formidable counter-attacker. Nadal's running lefty forehand was off. Most importantly, his spirit was broken. Trailing two sets to one, tied at 1-1 in the fourth set, Nadal lost 20 of the last 21 points as Blake rolled to a 6-4, 4-6, 6-3, 6-1 triumph.

As Blake reflected on his win, he was very appreciative of how fervently the fans got behind him. "The crowd was unbelievable," he said. "A few times — on break points, set points and on match point — when they were screaming and getting on their feet, I really couldn't hear a thing ... You try not to think of the magnitude of 20-some-odd-thousand people screaming for you. It was amazing."

When Blake took on Agassi in the match of the tournament, under the lights in the quarters, the crowd was torn. Many fans leaned toward Blake, sympathizing with his plight. More were on the side of Agassi, an American icon, the man they had been watching for two decades. Only once in four previous encounters had Blake beaten his one-time idol, and that, too, was a battle fought in the evening on hard courts in Washington three years ago. It was after 10 p.m. when Blake and Agassi took the court this time.

Appearing in his first career quarterfinal at a Grand Slam event, Blake came out blazing, blasting winners off both flanks, puncturing holes in Agassi's second serve, serving with immense power and deception. Blake swept through the first two sets and went up a break at 3-2 in the third, then played a loose game on his serve. Agassi pounced, winning four consecutive games to take that set. In the fourth, Blake, who had been so energized and inspired, was deflated and debilitated.

But a revitalized Blake struck back audaciously in the fifth set. He served for the match at 5-4. As the players came back on court before the start of the 10th game, the vociferous crowd understood Agassi might be on his way out of the Open, perhaps permanently. They chanted: "Andre! Andre! Andre!" to get him fired up. Blake got to 15-0, but never won another point. Agassi characteristically went after his returns and Blake did not assert himself. On they traveled to a stirring tie-break conclusion, and once more, Blake seemed poised for victory when he took a 3-0 lead, later serving with a 5-4 advantage. Agassi came out of that corner to reach match point at 6-5, but Blake saved it with a sizzling forehand winner. It was 6-6, but two points later Agassi finished off the suspenseful showdown with a gutsy forehand return winner of his own, coming through 3-6, 3-6, 6-3, 6-3, 7-6 (6).

Agassi demonstrated extraordinary grit and gumption in staging his sixth career comeback from two-sets-to-love down. Agassi was commendable, but Blake let a major opportunity slip from his grasp, and his five-set record dropped to 0-6. Had he won this match, he might well have ousted Ginepri to reach his first final at a major, and that could have propelled him to another level. But, perhaps, part of his problem was having too much respect for Agassi. The loss did not seem to sting as much as it should have. Blake has a history of difficulty closing out matches, and this one might haunt him for a long while.

Clearly, Roddick was haunted by his opening round departure at the hands of Gilles Muller, the left-hander from Luxembourg. Muller can be dangerous. He stopped Nadal at Wimbledon, beat

Agassi in the summer of 2004 and got to the final of Los Angeles this season. The fact remained that the fourth-seeded Roddick was facing the world's 68th-ranked player, a streaky competitor who had failed to qualify for two Masters Series events over the summer. Roddick, meanwhile, had not only captured his one and only major title at the Open in 2003, but in the previous four years had not bowed out earlier than the quarterfinals.

This time around, he could not come to terms with Muller's wicked slice serve and his array of spins and speeds. Roddick kept retreating further behind the baseline for his returns and the move got him nowhere. The 23-year-old American — playing, in fact, on his birthday — let himself down by losing three consecutive tie-breaks to fall 7-6 (4), 7-6 (8), 7-6 (1), continuing his pattern of falling short in crucial tie-breaks. He lost two in the course of a four-set loss to Hewitt this year in the semifinals of the Australian Open, and dropped the second-set tie-break in his straight sets loss to Federer in the Wimbledon final. After breaking Muller (who was taken apart easily by Ginepri in the following round) early in the first set, he never did so again. Roddick lost control of this match when he inexplicably dropped a love service game at 5-3 in the first set. His lack of intensity there was fatal. Two years have passed without Roddick collecting a second Grand Slam tournament crown. He will be hard pressed to garner his next one.

Clearly, this was a terrible setback for Roddick, a defeat he never expected would occur. As he lamented, "I don't remember a loss where I've felt this bad afterward. ...I've never cared so much as I care right now, which makes it tough. I just killed it this year as far as working hard, doing all the right things. ...I can blame myself because I was in control and then I let him back in."

In the end, of course, Roddick was long gone by the time Federer claimed the crown. Now he is tied for Grand Slam tournament singles championships with Boris Becker and Stefan Edberg at six, although no one but Federer has ever reached that mark without losing a final. It won't be long before he moves past the likes of John McEnroe and Mats Wilander (seven each); Jimmy Connors, Agassi, and Ivan Lendl (eight); and then starts closing in on double digits. All of the game's closest observers will follow his progress with special interest over the next couple of seasons.

But the cognoscenti will also be wondering if Agassi will play the 2006 U.S. Open or even another Grand Slam event. He has not garnered a major since the Australian Open of 2003, and although he was genuinely gratified about making it to the Open final, it is hard to imagine Agassi accepting noble defeats in big finals for much longer. He seems conflicted about whether to keep going after a year requiring cortisone shots to treat his problem with sciatica. As he says, "I'm unsure what I'm going to do in a month, let alone a year from now. But as of now my intention is to keep working and keep doing what it is I do. The only thing better than the last 20 years will be the last 21 years."

JAMES BLAKE

JAMES BLAKE (FOREGROUND) AND RAFAEL NADAL

nase

MARY
COHR

GUILLERMO CORIA

GUILLERMO CORIA

TAYLOR DENT

DAVID NALBANDIAN

org

RAFAEL NADAL

Thai
adidas

PARADORN SRICHAPHAN

ANDY RODDICK

DONALD YOUNG

ROGER FEDERER

2005 U.S. OPEN MEN'S SINGLES

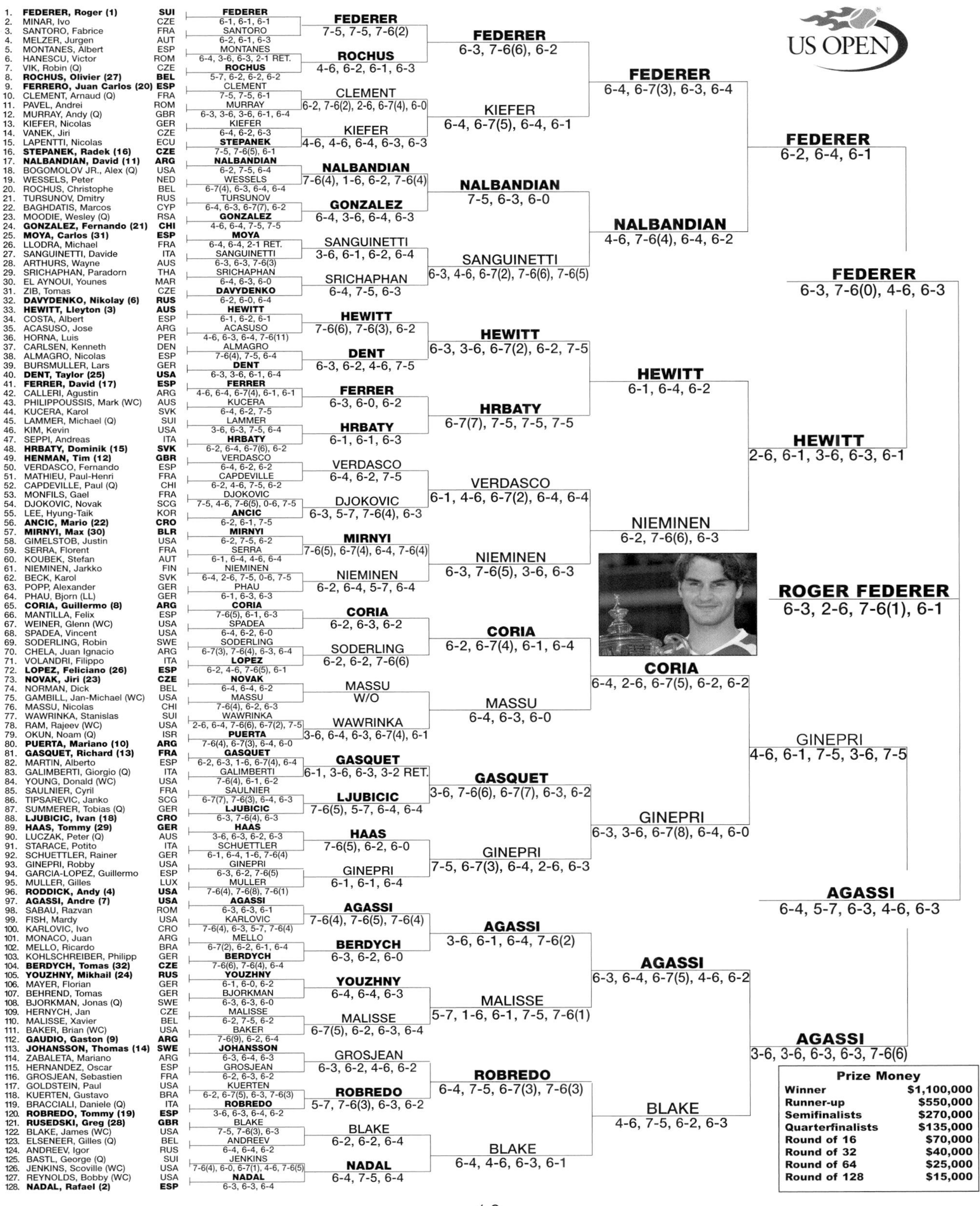

1.	**FEDERER, Roger (1)**	**SUI**
2.	MINAR, Ivo	CZE
3.	SANTORO, Fabrice	FRA
4.	MELZER, Jurgen	AUT
5.	MONTANES, Albert	ESP
6.	HANESCU, Victor	ROM
7.	VIK, Robin (Q)	CZE
8.	**ROCHUS, Olivier (27)**	**BEL**
9.	**FERRERO, Juan Carlos (20)**	**ESP**
10.	CLEMENT, Arnaud (Q)	FRA
11.	PAVEL, Andrei	ROM
12.	MURRAY, Andy (Q)	GBR
13.	KIEFER, Nicolas	GER
14.	VANEK, Jiri	CZE
15.	LAPENTTI, Nicolas	ECU
16.	**STEPANEK, Radek (16)**	**CZE**
17.	**NALBANDIAN, David (11)**	**ARG**
18.	BOGOMOLOV JR., Alex (Q)	USA
19.	WESSELS, Peter	NED
20.	ROCHUS, Christophe	BEL
21.	TURSUNOV, Dmitry	RUS
22.	BAGHDATIS, Marcos	CYP
23.	MOODIE, Wesley (Q)	RSA
24.	**GONZALEZ, Fernando (21)**	**CHI**
25.	**MOYA, Carlos (31)**	**ESP**
26.	LLODRA, Michael	FRA
27.	SANGUINETTI, Davide	ITA
28.	ARTHURS, Wayne	AUS
29.	SRICHAPHAN, Paradorn	THA
30.	EL AYNOUI, Younes	MAR
31.	ZIB, Tomas	CZE
32.	**DAVYDENKO, Nikolay (6)**	**RUS**
33.	**HEWITT, Lleyton (3)**	**AUS**
34.	COSTA, Albert	ESP
35.	ACASUSO, Jose	ARG
36.	HORNA, Luis	PER
37.	CARLSEN, Kenneth	DEN
38.	ALMAGRO, Nicolas	ESP
39.	BURSMULLER, Lars	GER
40.	**DENT, Taylor (25)**	**USA**
41.	**FERRER, David (17)**	**ESP**
42.	CALLERI, Agustin	ARG
43.	PHILIPPOUSSIS, Mark (WC)	AUS
44.	KUCERA, Karol	SVK
45.	LAMMER, Michael (Q)	SUI
46.	KIM, Kevin	USA
47.	SEPPI, Andreas	ITA
48.	**HRBATY, Dominik (15)**	**SVK**
49.	**HENMAN, Tim (12)**	**GBR**
50.	VERDASCO, Fernando	ESP
51.	MATHIEU, Paul-Henri	FRA
52.	CAPDEVILLE, Paul (Q)	CHI
53.	MONFILS, Gael	FRA
54.	DJOKOVIC, Novak	SCG
55.	LEE, Hyung-Taik	KOR
56.	**ANCIC, Mario (22)**	**CRO**
57.	**MIRNYI, Max (30)**	**BLR**
58.	GIMELSTOB, Justin	USA
59.	SERRA, Florent	FRA
60.	KOUBEK, Stefan	AUT
61.	NIEMINEN, Jarkko	FIN
62.	BECK, Karol	SVK
63.	POPP, Alexander	GER
64.	PHAU, Bjorn (LL)	GER
65.	**CORIA, Guillermo (8)**	**ARG**
66.	MANTILLA, Felix	ESP
67.	WEINER, Glenn (WC)	USA
68.	SPADEA, Vincent	USA
69.	SODERLING, Robin	SWE
70.	CHELA, Juan Ignacio	ARG
71.	VOLANDRI, Filippo	ITA
72.	**LOPEZ, Feliciano (26)**	**ESP**
73.	**NOVAK, Jiri (23)**	**CZE**
74.	NORMAN, Dick	BEL
75.	GAMBILL, Jan-Michael (WC)	USA
76.	MASSU, Nicolas	CHI
77.	WAWRINKA, Stanislas	SUI
78.	RAM, Rajeev (WC)	USA
79.	OKUN, Noam (Q)	ISR
80.	**PUERTA, Mariano (10)**	**ARG**
81.	**GASQUET, Richard (13)**	**FRA**
82.	MARTIN, Alberto	ESP
83.	GALIMBERTI, Giorgio (Q)	ITA
84.	YOUNG, Donald (WC)	USA
85.	SAULNIER, Cyril	FRA
86.	TIPSAREVIC, Janko	SCG
87.	SUMMERER, Tobias (Q)	GER
88.	**LJUBICIC, Ivan (18)**	**CRO**
89.	**HAAS, Tommy (29)**	**GER**
90.	LUCZAK, Peter (Q)	AUS
91.	STARACE, Potito	ITA
92.	SCHUETTLER, Rainer	GER
93.	GINEPRI, Robby	USA
94.	GARCIA-LOPEZ, Guillermo	ESP
95.	MULLER, Gilles	LUX
96.	**RODDICK, Andy (4)**	**USA**
97.	**AGASSI, Andre (7)**	**USA**
98.	SABAU, Razvan	ROM
99.	FISH, Mardy	USA
100.	KARLOVIC, Ivo	CRO
101.	MONACO, Juan	ARG
102.	MELLO, Ricardo	BRA
103.	KOHLSCHREIBER, Philipp	GER
104.	**BERDYCH, Tomas (32)**	**CZE**
105.	**YOUZHNY, Mikhail (24)**	**RUS**
106.	MAYER, Florian	GER
107.	BEHREND, Tomas	GER
108.	BJORKMAN, Jonas (Q)	SWE
109.	HERNYCH, Jan	CZE
110.	MALISSE, Xavier	BEL
111.	BAKER, Brian (WC)	USA
112.	**GAUDIO, Gaston (9)**	**ARG**
113.	**JOHANSSON, Thomas (14)**	**SWE**
114.	ZABALETA, Mariano	ARG
115.	HERNANDEZ, Oscar	ESP
116.	GROSJEAN, Sebastien	FRA
117.	GOLDSTEIN, Paul	USA
118.	KUERTEN, Gustavo	BRA
119.	BRACCIALI, Daniele (Q)	ITA
120.	**ROBREDO, Tommy (19)**	**ESP**
121.	**RUSEDSKI, Greg (28)**	**GBR**
122.	BLAKE, James (WC)	USA
123.	ELSENEER, Gilles (Q)	BEL
124.	ANDREEV, Igor	RUS
125.	BASTL, George (Q)	SUI
126.	JENKINS, Scoville (WC)	USA
127.	REYNOLDS, Bobby (WC)	USA
128.	**NADAL, Rafael (2)**	**ESP**

FEDERER 6-1, 6-1, 6-1
SANTORO 6-2, 6-1, 6-3
MONTANES 6-4, 3-6, 6-3, 2-1 RET.
ROCHUS 5-7, 6-2, 6-2, 6-2
CLEMENT 7-5, 7-5, 6-1
MURRAY 6-3, 3-6, 3-6, 6-1, 6-4
KIEFER 6-4, 6-2, 6-3
STEPANEK 7-5, 7-6(5), 6-1
NALBANDIAN 6-2, 7-5, 6-4
WESSELS 6-7(4), 6-3, 6-4, 6-4
TURSUNOV 6-4, 6-3, 6-7(7), 6-2
GONZALEZ 4-6, 6-4, 7-5, 7-5
MOYA 6-4, 6-4, 2-1 RET.
SANGUINETTI 6-3, 6-3, 7-6(3)
SRICHAPHAN 6-4, 6-3, 6-0
DAVYDENKO 6-2, 6-0, 6-4
HEWITT 6-1, 6-2, 6-1
ACASUSO 4-6, 6-3, 6-4, 7-6(11)
ALMAGRO 7-6(4), 7-5, 6-4
DENT 6-3, 3-6, 6-1, 6-4
FERRER 4-6, 6-4, 6-7(4), 6-1, 6-1
KUCERA 6-4, 6-2, 7-5
LAMMER 3-6, 6-3, 7-5, 6-4
HRBATY 6-2, 6-4, 6-7(6), 6-2
VERDASCO 6-4, 6-2, 6-2
CAPDEVILLE 6-2, 4-6, 7-5, 6-2
DJOKOVIC 7-5, 4-6, 7-6(5), 0-6, 7-5
ANCIC 6-2, 6-1, 7-5
MIRNYI 6-2, 7-5, 6-2
SERRA 6-1, 6-4, 4-6, 6-4
NIEMINEN 6-4, 2-6, 7-5, 0-6, 7-5
PHAU 6-1, 6-3, 6-3
CORIA 7-6(5), 6-1, 6-3
SPADEA 6-4, 6-2, 6-0
SODERLING 6-7(3), 7-6(4), 6-3, 6-4
LOPEZ 6-2, 4-6, 7-6(5), 6-1
NOVAK 6-4, 6-4, 6-2
MASSU 7-6(4), 6-2, 6-3
WAWRINKA 2-6, 6-4, 7-6(6), 6-7(2), 7-5
PUERTA 7-6(4), 6-7(3), 6-4, 6-0
GASQUET 6-2, 6-3, 1-6, 6-7(4), 6-4
GALIMBERTI 7-6(4), 6-1, 6-2
SAULNIER 6-7(7), 7-6(3), 6-4, 6-3
LJUBICIC 6-3, 7-6(4), 6-3
HAAS 3-6, 6-3, 6-2, 6-3
SCHUETTLER 6-1, 6-4, 1-6, 7-6(4)
GINEPRI 6-3, 6-2, 7-6(5)
MULLER 7-6(4), 7-6(8), 7-6(1)
AGASSI 6-3, 6-3, 6-1
KARLOVIC 7-6(4), 6-3, 5-7, 7-6(4)
MELLO 6-7(2), 6-2, 6-1, 6-4
BERDYCH 7-6(6), 7-6(4), 6-4
YOUZHNY 6-1, 6-0, 6-2
BJORKMAN 6-3, 6-3, 6-0
MALISSE 6-2, 7-5, 6-2
BAKER 7-6(9), 6-2, 6-4
JOHANSSON 6-3, 6-4, 6-3
GROSJEAN 6-2, 6-3, 6-2
KUERTEN 6-2, 6-7(5), 6-3, 7-6(3)
ROBREDO 3-6, 6-3, 6-4, 6-2
BLAKE 7-5, 7-6(3), 6-3
ANDREEV 6-4, 6-4, 6-2
JENKINS 7-6(4), 6-0, 6-7(1), 4-6, 7-6(5)
NADAL 6-3, 6-3, 6-4

FEDERER 7-5, 7-5, 7-6(2)
ROCHUS 4-6, 6-2, 6-1, 6-3
CLEMENT 6-2, 7-6(2), 2-6, 6-7(4), 6-0
KIEFER 4-6, 4-6, 6-4, 6-3, 6-3
NALBANDIAN 7-6(4), 1-6, 6-2, 7-6(4)
GONZALEZ 6-4, 3-6, 6-4, 6-3
SANGUINETTI 3-6, 6-1, 6-2, 6-4
SRICHAPHAN 6-4, 7-5, 6-3
HEWITT 7-6(6), 7-6(3), 6-2
DENT 6-3, 6-2, 4-6, 7-5
FERRER 6-3, 6-0, 6-2
HRBATY 6-1, 6-1, 6-3
VERDASCO 6-4, 6-2, 7-5
DJOKOVIC 6-3, 5-7, 7-6(4), 6-3
MIRNYI 7-6(5), 6-7(4), 6-4, 7-6(4)
NIEMINEN 6-2, 6-4, 5-7, 6-4
CORIA 6-2, 6-3, 6-2
SODERLING 6-2, 6-2, 7-6(6)
MASSU W/O
WAWRINKA 3-6, 6-4, 6-3, 6-7(4), 6-1
GASQUET 6-1, 3-6, 6-3, 3-2 RET.
LJUBICIC 7-6(5), 5-7, 6-4, 6-4
HAAS 7-6(5), 6-2, 6-0
GINEPRI 6-1, 6-1, 6-4
AGASSI 7-6(4), 7-6(5), 7-6(4)
BERDYCH 6-3, 6-2, 6-0
YOUZHNY 6-4, 6-4, 6-3
MALISSE 6-7(5), 6-2, 6-3, 6-4
GROSJEAN 6-3, 6-2, 4-6, 6-2
ROBREDO 5-7, 7-6(3), 6-3, 6-2
BLAKE 6-2, 6-2, 6-4
NADAL 6-4, 7-5, 6-4

FEDERER 6-3, 7-6(6), 6-2
KIEFER 6-4, 6-7(5), 6-4, 6-1
NALBANDIAN 7-5, 6-3, 6-0
SANGUINETTI 6-3, 4-6, 6-7(2), 7-6(6), 7-6(5)
HEWITT 6-3, 3-6, 6-7(2), 6-2, 7-5
HRBATY 6-7(7), 7-5, 7-5, 7-5
VERDASCO 6-1, 4-6, 6-7(2), 6-4, 6-4
NIEMINEN 6-3, 7-6(5), 3-6, 6-3
CORIA 6-2, 6-7(4), 6-1, 6-4
MASSU 6-4, 6-3, 6-0
GASQUET 3-6, 7-6(6), 6-7(7), 6-3, 6-2
GINEPRI 7-5, 6-7(3), 6-4, 2-6, 6-3
AGASSI 3-6, 6-1, 6-4, 7-6(2)
MALISSE 5-7, 1-6, 6-1, 7-5, 7-6(1)
ROBREDO 6-4, 7-5, 6-7(3), 7-6(3)
BLAKE 6-4, 4-6, 6-3, 6-1

FEDERER 6-4, 6-7(3), 6-3, 6-4
NALBANDIAN 4-6, 7-6(4), 6-4, 6-2
HEWITT 6-1, 6-4, 6-2
NIEMINEN 6-2, 7-6(6), 6-3
CORIA 6-4, 2-6, 6-7(5), 6-2, 6-2
GINEPRI 6-3, 3-6, 6-7(8), 6-4, 6-0
AGASSI 6-3, 6-4, 6-7(5), 4-6, 6-2
BLAKE 4-6, 7-5, 6-2, 6-3

FEDERER 6-2, 6-4, 6-1
HEWITT 2-6, 6-1, 3-6, 6-3, 6-1
GINEPRI 4-6, 6-1, 7-5, 3-6, 7-5
AGASSI 3-6, 3-6, 6-3, 6-3, 7-6(6)

FEDERER 6-3, 7-6(0), 4-6, 6-3
AGASSI 6-4, 5-7, 6-3, 4-6, 6-3

ROGER FEDERER 6-3, 2-6, 7-6(1), 6-1

Prize Money

Winner	**$1,100,000**
Runner-up	**$550,000**
Semifinalists	**$270,000**
Quarterfinalists	**$135,000**
Round of 16	**$70,000**
Round of 32	**$40,000**
Round of 64	**$25,000**
Round of 128	**$15,000**

MIKE BRYAN (l) AND BOB BRYAN (r)

U.S. OPEN MEN'S DOUBLES

PRIZE MONEY			
Winner	$400,000	Quarterfinalists	$50,000
Finalist	$200,000	Round of 16	$25,000
Semifinalists	$100,000	Round of 32	$15,000
		Round of 64	$10,000

First Round

- **BJORKMAN, J. (SWE)/MIRNYI, M. (BLR) (1)**
- MARTIN, A. (ESP)/ZIB, T. (CZE)
- BAKER, B./RAM, R. (USA) (WC)
- JENKINS, S./REYNOLDS, B. (USA) (WC)
- HAAS, T./WASKE, A. (GER)
- KUZNETSOV, A./OUDSEMA, S. (USA) (WC)
- LOPEZ, F./VERDASCO, F. (ESP)
- **ETLIS, G./RODRIGUEZ, M. (ARG) (14)**
- **SUK, C./VIZNER, P. (CZE) (12)**
- CALATRAVA, A./FERRER, D. (ESP)
- ALLEGRO, Y. (SUI)/BRACCIALI, D. (ITA)
- EL AYNAOUI, Y. (MAR)/VANHOUDT, T. (BEL)
- PAVEL, A. (ROM)/SCHUETTLER, R. (GER)
- HERNYCH, J. (CZE)/SPADEA, V. (USA)
- KNOWLE, J./MELZER, J. (AUT)
- **LLODRA, M./SANTORO, F. (FRA) (6)**
- **BLACK, W./ULLYETT, K. (ZIM) (4)**
- GALIMBERTI, G. (ITA)/SRICHAPHAN, P. (THA)
- BERTOLINI, M./VOLANDRI, F. (ITA)
- QUERREY, S./YOUNG, D. (USA) (WC)
- CHELA, J.I./ZABALETA, M. (ARG)
- JOHANSSON, T. (SWE)/KOENIG, R. (RSA)
- PALMER, J./PARROTT, T. (USA)
- **ARNOLD, L. (ARG)/PALA, P. (CZE) (16)**
- **ERLICH, J./RAM, A. (ISR) (11)**
- CIBULEC, T./NOVAK, J. (CZE)
- HANESCU, V./SABAU, R. (ROM)
- GIMELSTOB, J. (USA)/HOOD, M. (ARG)
- KERR, J. (AUS)/OLIVER, G. (USA)
- BERDYCH, T. (CZE)/MAYER, F. (GER)
- DELIC, A./MORRISON, J. (USA) (WC)
- **PAES, L. (IND)/ZIMONJIC, N. (SCG) (5)**
- **BHUPATHI, M. (IND)/DAMM, M. (CZE) (7)**
- MONFILS, G./SAULNIER, C. (FRA)
- ANCIC, M./LJUBICIC, I. (CRO)
- SKOCH, D./STEPANEK, R. (CZE)
- ROCHUS, C. (BEL/WAWRINKA, S. (SUI)
- ANDREEV, R./DAVYDENKO, N. (RUS)
- FISHER, A. (AUS)/LEACH, R. (USA)
- **ASPELIN, S. (SWE)/PERRY, T. (AUS) (9)**
- **HUSS, S. (AUS)/MOODIE, W. (RSA) (13)**
- BURGSMULLER, L. (GER)/YOUZHNY, M. (RUS)
- BOGOMOLOV JR., A./RETTENMAIER, T. (USA) (WC)
- BECK, K. (SVK)/LEVINSKY, J. (CZE)
- KRYVONOS, M./ZIVKOVIC, D. (USA) (WC)
- ACASUSO, J./PRIETO, S. (ARG)
- GOLDSTEIN, P./THOMAS, J. (USA)
- **KNOWLES, M. (BAH)/NESTOR, D. (CAN) (3)**
- **ARTHURS, W./HANLEY, P. (AUS) (8)**
- NIEMINEN, J. (FIN)/WASSEN, R. (NED)
- HRBATY, D./MERTINAK, M. (SVK)
- FYRSTENBERG, M./MATKOWSKI, M. (POL)
- BENNETEAU, J./MAHUT, N. (FRA)
- GARCIA, M. (ARG)/HORNA, L. (PER)
- GINEPRI, R. (USA)/MULLER, G. (LUX)
- **CERMAK, F./FRIEDL, L. (CZE) (10)**
- **GONZALEZ, F./MASSU, N. (CHI) (15)**
- KOHLSCHREIBER, P. (GER)/ROCHUS, O. (BEL)
- CARLSEN, K. (DEN)/COETZEE, J. (RSA)
- ARTONI, E. (ITA)/PUERTA, M. (ARG)
- SANGUINETTI, D./SEPPI, A. (ITA)
- LINDSTEDT, R./SODERLING, R. (SWE)
- CLEMENT, A./GROSJEAN, S. (FRA)
- **BRYAN, B./BRYAN, M. (USA) (2)**

Second Round

- **BJORKMAN/MIRNYI** 6-0, 6-3
- JENKINS/REYNOLDS 6-1, 3-6, 6-3
- KUZNETSOV/OUDSEMA 7-6(6), 6-3
- LOPEZ/VERDASCO 7-6(4), 3-6, 7-6(3)
- **SUK/VIZNER** 6-3, 6-1
- ALLEGRO/BRACCIALI 6-3, 6-3
- HERNYCH/SPADEA 7-6(2), 6-2
- KNOWLE/MELZER 3-6, 7-6(0), 6-4
- **BLACK/ULLYETT** 6-3, 7-5
- BERTOLINI/VOLANDRI 6-2, 6-4
- JOHANSSON/KOENIG 6-3, 6-4
- PALMER/PARROTT 7-5, 6-4
- **ERLICH/RAM** 3-2 RET.
- HANESCU/SABAU 2-6, 7-5, 6-4
- KERR/OLIVER 6-4, 6-4
- DELIC/MORRISON 7-6(6), 7-6(2)
- **BHUPATHI/DAMM** 6-1, 6-3
- ANCIC/LJUBICIC 6-2, 7-6(0)
- ANDREEV/DAVYDENKO 7-5, 6-1
- **ASPELIN/PERRY** 5-7, 6-2, 7-6(3)
- BURGSMULLER/YOUZHNY 7-6(7), 6-1
- BECK/LEVINSKY 6-2, 6-3
- ACASUSO/PRIETO 6-4, 6-4
- GOLDSTEIN/THOMAS 4-6, 6-4, 6-2
- **ARTHURS/HANLEY** 7-5, 6-3
- HRBATY/MERTINAK 4-6, 6-3, 6-4
- BENNETEAU/MAHUT 6-4, 6-4
- **CERMAK/FRIEDL** 6-4, 6-3
- **GONZALEZ/MASSU** 6-4, 7-6(0)
- CARLSEN/COETZEE 6-2, 6-3
- LINDSTEDT/SODERLING 6-3, 6-1
- **BRYAN/BRYAN** 7-6(5), 1-6, 6-3

Third Round

- **BJORKMAN/MIRNYI** 6-7(3), 6-2, 6-1
- LOPEZ/VERDASCO 6-7(1), 6-4, 6-4
- **SUK/VIZNER** 6-3, 2-6, 6-3
- HERNYCH/SPADEA 7-6(2), 4-6, 7-5
- **BLACK/ULLYETT** 6-2, 6-0
- JOHANSSON/KOENIG 6-3, 6-2
- **ERLICH/RAM** 6-0, 6-2
- DELIC/MORRISON 7-5, 7-5
- **BHUPATHI/DAMM** 7-6(3), 3-6, 7-6(6)
- **ASPELIN/PERRY** 6-1, 6-1
- BURGSMULLER/YOUZHNY 6-4, 6-2
- GOLDSTEIN/THOMAS 6-0, 6-3
- **ARTHURS/HANLEY** 6-3, 6-2
- BENNETEAU/MAHUT 7-5, 7-6(6)
- **GONZALEZ/MASSU** 6-4, 6-4
- **BRYAN/BRYAN** 4-6, 6-2, 6-3

Quarterfinals

- **BJORKMAN/MIRNYI** 6-3, 6-4
- **SUK/VIZNER** 7-6(7), 6-4
- **BLACK/ULLYETT** 4-6, 6-0, 6-1
- **ERLICH/RAM** 7-6(3), 6-3
- **ASPELIN/PERRY** 6-4, 6-7(3), 6-3
- GOLDSTEIN/THOMAS 7-6(8), 6-2
- BENNETEAU/MAHUT 6-4, 7-6(6)
- **BRYAN/BRYAN** 6-3, 6-1

Semifinals

- **BJORKMAN/MIRNYI** 6-4, 6-3
- **BLACK/ULLYETT** 6-4, 6-2
- GOLDSTEIN/THOMAS 4-6, 6-4, 7-6(14)
- **BRYAN/BRYAN** 6-3, 6-4

Final

- **BJORKMAN/MIRNYI** 5-7, 7-5, 6-2
- **BRYAN/BRYAN** 3-6, 6-1, 6-2

Champions

BRYAN/BRYAN 6-1, 6-4

005 U.S. OPEN MEN'S & WOMEN'S QUALIFYING

Men's Qualifying

IK, Robin (1)	**CZE**
IEALEY, Nathan	AUS
OJER, Jean-Julien	AHO
ETTENMAIER, Travis (WC)	USA
E VOEST, Rik	RSA
ONZALEZ, Santiago	MEX
HERWOOD, David	GBR
UKSAR, Sasa (31)	**CRO**
RACCIALI, Daniele (2)	**ITA**
ABASHVILI, Teimuraz	RUS
EVY, Harel	ISR
EMIC, Dusan	SCG
ERRER, Michael	GER
OLTCHKOV, Vladimir	BLR
LESS, Kristian	DEN
ARANUSIC, Roko (23)	**CRO**
LEMENT, Arnaud (3)	**FRA**
HEN, Ti (A)	TPE
TAKHOVSKY, Sergiy	UKR
ARRAZ, Gregory	FRA
EVILDER, Nicolas	FRA
AN SCHEPPINGEN, Dennis	NED
ENCONI, Tomas	ITA
DOMCHOKE, Danai (21)	**THA**
LOUHY, Lukas (4)	**CZE**
ARSTRAND, Marcus	SWE
EQUERY, Jean-Michel	FRA
LSENEER, Gilles	BEL
MRITRAJ, Prakash	IND
IAHUT, Nicolas	FRA
VANS, Brendan (WC)	USA
IERTINAK, Michal (24)	**SVK**
SCIONE, Thierry (5)	**FRA**
IARRAY, Jonathan	GBR
ILLAGRAN, Cristian	ARG
LVES, Thiago	BRA
ARCIA, Adrian	CHI
ILVA, Julio	BRA
UCZAK, Peter	AUS
LIEGEN, Kristof (17)	**BEL**
ARETTA, Flavio (6)	**BRA**
ALLARDO VALLES, Miguel	MEX
UMMERER, Tobias	GER
UZZI, Federico	ITA
ODERO, Nicolas	ARG
LEISHMAN, Zack (WC)	USA
AHALY, Brian	USA
U, Yen-Hsun (19)	**TPE**
HAU, Bjorn (7)	**GER**
EVINE, Jesse (WC)	USA
UCCIONE, Chris	AUS
UBOT, Lukasz	POL
APDEVILLE, Paul	CHI
CHUKIN, Yuri	RUS
LAYTON, Alex (WC)	USA
ANIEL, Marcos (28)	**BRA**
IMON, Gilles (8)	**FRA**
IIRANDA, Ivan	PER
E CHAUNAC, Sebastien	FRA
IENER, Glenn	USA
ARMAR, Arvind	GBR
HADAJ, Adam	POL
RMANDO, Hugo	USA
ALATRAVA, Alex (26)	**ESP**
OODIE, Wesley (9)	**RSA**
ASSON, Jeroen	BEL
OGER-VASSELIN, Edouard	FRA
NOBEL, Pavel	CZE
ILYNARIK, Zbynek	AUT
ANCEVIC, Frank	CAN
UZUKI, Takao	JPN
ISNARD, Jean-Rene (18)	**FRA**
JORKMAN, Jonas (10)	**SWE**
ARTFIELD, Diego	ARG
EL POTRO, Juan Martin	ARG
ELGADO, Ramon	PAR
ALVANI, Stefano	ITA
RPIC, Filip	SWE
IMMICH, Marc	AUS
ATIENCE, Olivier (27)	**FRA**
ABARA, Michal (11)	**CZE**
ALLA, Alejandro	COL
RUTTERO, John Paul (WC)	USA
AMMER, Michael	SUI
DESNIK, Wayne (WC)	USA
P DER HEIJDE, Melvyn	NED
REMELMAYR, Denis	GER
REUL, Simon (20)	**GER**
ASKE, Alexander (12)	**GER**
OGOMOLOV JR, Alex	USA
IAMIIT, Cecil	USA
AKL, Tomas	CZE
ANKAD, Harsh	IND
MYCZEK, Tim (WC)	USA
ILTON, Mark	GBR
ENNETEAU, Julien (25)	**FRA**
ASTL, George (13)	**SUI**
OITMAN, Sergio	ARG
EUBERGER, Ivo	SUI
EHNQUIST, Bjorn	SWE
QUILLARI, Franco	ARG
MEETS, Robert	AUS
ICQUEL, Marc	FRA
RZEZICKI, Juan Pablo (30)	**ARG**
UPUIS, Antony (14)	**FRA**
UERREY, Sam (WC)	USA
TOPPINI, Andrea	ITA
IORRISON, Jeff	USA
ERREIRO, Franco	BRA
OLELLI, Simone	ITA
ALIMBERTI, Giorgio	ITA
A, Andre (29)	**BRA**
IURRAY, Andy (15)	**GBR**
ELA, Dudi	ISR
DAKTUSSON, Jacob	SWE
ORENZI, Paolo	ITA
RUTHANS, Victor	SVK
UNITSYN, Igor	RUS
ERGEA, Florin	ROM
APENTTI, Giovanni (22)	**ECU**
ANG, Yeu-Tzuoo (16)	**TPE**
ELGADO, Jamie	GBR
IEMEYER, Frederic	CAN
KUN, Noam	ISR
EYA, Alexander	AUT
ACEK, Jan	CZE
OGDANOVIC, Alex	GBR
ELIC, Amer (32)	**USA**

First Round

Winner	Score
VIK	6-2, 7-5
RETTENMAIER	6-4, 6-3
DE VOEST	6-0, 6-3
TUKSAR	3-6, 7-6(5), 6-1
BRACCIALI	6-4, 6-4
LEVY	6-4, 6-2
BERRER	7-6(5), 7-5
PLESS	6-4, 6-2
CLEMENT	6-2, 6-1
STAKHOVSKY	5-7, 6-3, 6-4
VAN SCHEPPINGEN	7-6(3), 7-6(4)
UDOMCHOKE	6-4, 6-4
DLOUHY	6-3, 6-4
ELSENEER	6-3, 6-0
AMRITRAJ	7-6(4), 6-4
MERTINAK	6-4, 6-4
MARRAY	4-6, 6-3, 6-2
ALVES	6-4, 4-6, 6-3
GARCIA	6-4, 6-0
LUCZAK	6-4, 6-2
SARETTA	6-1, 6-1
SUMMERER	4-6, 6-1, 6-1
FLEISHMAN	6-1, 7-5
LU	5-7, 6-2, 6-2
PHAU	6-4, 6-2
KUBOT	7-6(5), 6-2
CAPDEVILLE	7-6(5), 6-3
DANIEL	6-4, 6-4
MIRANDA	4-6, 6-4, 7-5
WEINER	7-5, 4-6, 6-1
PARMAR	6-3, 6-0
ARMANDO	6-3, 6-4
MOODIE	6-2, 6-2
ROGER-VASSELIN	7-5, 6-3
DANCEVIC	6-4, 6-7(5), 7-6(2)
LISNARD	6-3, 6-3
BJORKMAN	6-3, 7-5
DELGADO	6-3, 6-2
GALVANI	7-5, 6-3
PATIENCE	5-2 RET.
TABARA	7-5, 7-6(1)
LAMMER	6-2, 6-4
ODESNIK	6-4, 6-3
GREMELMAYR	6-4, 6-1
BOGOMOLOV JR.	6-4, 7-6(11)
MAMIIT	6-2, 7-6(11)
MANKAD	6-3, 6-2
BENNETEAU	6-4, 7-5
BASTL	6-3, 1-6, 7-6(5)
HEUBERGER	3-6, 6-2, 6-1
SQUILLARI	6-2, 6-4
BRZEZICKI	6-3, 1-6, 6-1
DUPUIS	6-4, 7-6(4)
STOPPINI	7-6(2), 6-2
BOLELLI	7-6(6), 7-6(4)
GALIMBERTI	5-7, 7-5, 6-2
MURRAY	6-4, 6-4
LORENZI	6-2, 7-6(2)
KUNITSYN	6-1, 4-1 RET.
LAPENTTI	5-7, 6-3, 6-4
WANG	6-3, 6-3
OKUN	6-4, 1-6, 6-1
PEYA	6-1, 3-6, 6-1
DELIC	6-4, 7-6(7)

Second Round

Winner	Score
VIK	7-5, 6-2
DE VOEST	7-6(5), 3-6, 6-2
BRACCIALI	5-7, 6-4, 7-6(3)
BERRER	6-1, 6-4
CLEMENT	1-6, 6-4, 6-4
UDOMCHOKE	7-5, 7-6(4)
ELSENEER	6-3, 6-3
MERTINAK	6-3, 6-1
ALVES	6-4, 6-2
LUCZAK	7-5, 4-6, 6-2
SUMMERER	2-6, 6-3, 7-5
LU	3-6, 6-4, 6-4
PHAU	6-4, 7-5
CAPDEVILLE	6-4, 6-3
WEINER	6-7(3), 6-2, 7-6(2)
ARMANDO	6-3, 6-4
MOODIE	6-2, 7-5
LISNARD	1-6, 6-4, 6-2
BJORKMAN	6-4, 6-3
GALVANI	6-3, 6-3
LAMMER	7-6(6), 2-6, 7-5
GREMELMAYR	6-2, 6-3
BOGOMOLOV JR.	3-6, 6-2, 7-5
BENNETEAU	6-3, 3-6, 6-4
BASTL	6-4, 2-6, 6-4
BRZEZICKI	6-4, 1-6, 7-6(5)
DUPUIS	4-6, 7-6(2), 7-6(4)
GALIMBERTI	6-4, 6-4
MURRAY	6-3, 6-2
LAPENTTI	3-6, 6-3, 6-3
OKUN	6-3, 1-6, 6-4
PEYA	6-4, 3-6, 7-6(7)

Final Round

Winner	Score
VIK	3-6, 6-2, 6-3
BRACCIALI	7-6(3), 7-6(2)
CLEMENT	0-6, 7-5, 7-6(4)
ELSENEER	6-4, 2-6, 6-4
LUCZAK	6-1, 6-4
SUMMERER	6-3, 6-1
CAPDEVILLE	6-4, 7-5
WEINER	6-7(5), 6-3, 6-4
MOODIE	6-7(1), 6-1, 6-1
BJORKMAN	6-1, 6-7(5), 6-0
LAMMER	6-4, 6-2
BOGOMOLOV JR	7-6(5), 7-5
BASTL	2-6, 6-2, 6-3
GALIMBERTI	7-6(6), 7-6(2)
MURRAY	6-0, 7-6(5)
OKUN	6-4, 6-7(7), 6-2

Women's Qualifying

1. **BAMMER, Sybille (1)**	**AUT**
2. LI, Ting	CHN
3. YAN, Zi	CHN
4. NEMECKOVA, Lenka	CZE
5. HENKE, Vanessa	GER
6. MAKAROVA, Ekaterina	RUS
7. BEYGELZIMER, Yulia	UKR
8. **UBEROI, Shikha (18)**	**IND**
9. **DOMINGUEZ LINO, L. (2)**	**ESP**
10. HOPKINS, Jennifer	USA
11. HISAMATSU, Shiho	JPN
12. UBEROI, Neha (WC)	USA
13. AMANMURADOVA, Akgul	UZB
14. KUTI-KIS, Rita	HUN
15. LISJAK, Ivana	CRO
16. **KLASCHKA, Sabine (29)**	**GER**
17. **SANCHEZ LORENZO, Maria (3)**	**USA**
18. O'DONOGHUE, Jane	GBR
19. SZAVAY, Agnes	HUN
20. SAVCHUK, Olga	UKR
21. CANEPA, Alice	ITA
22. GUBACSI, Zsofia	HUN
23. DRAKE, Maureen	CAN
24. **LAINE, Emma (17)**	**FIN**
25. **PIRONKOVA, Tszvetana (4)**	**BUL**
26. BLAHOTOVA, Olga	CZE
27. DABEK, Tiffany	USA
28. BOHMOVA, Katerina	CZE
29. GEHRLEIN, Stephanie	GER
30. HRADECKA, Lucie	CZE
31. PIEDAD, Frederica	POR
32. **ALVES, Maria Fernanda (32)**	**BRA**
33. **ARVIDSSON, Sofia (5)**	**SWE**
34. ANTYPINA, Olena	UKR
35. WEINGARTNER, Marlene	GER
36. SUN, Tian-Tian	CHN
37. SERRA ZANETTI, Adriana	ITA
38. PRUSOVA, Libuse	CZE
39. FISLOVA, Eva	SVK
40. **CERVANOVA, Ludmila (23)**	**SVK**
41. **SROMOVA, Hana (6)**	**CZE**
42. OBATA, Saori	JPN
43. MARCIO, Krysty (WC)	USA
44. HSIEH, Su-Wei	TPE
45. SEQUERA, Milagros	VEN
46. TAMAELA, Elise	NED
47. NOCIAROVA, Dominika	SVK
48. **MARRERO, Marta (22)**	**ESP**
49. **KLOESEL, Sandra (7)**	**GER**
50. JOHANSSON, Mathilde	FRA
51. STANCIUTE, Lina	LTU
52. BACHMANN, Angelika	GER
53. SCHAUL, Claudine	LUX
54. SESCIOREANU, Delia	ROM
55. BARNA, Adriana	GER
56. **TU, Meilen (31)**	**USA**
57. **RUANO PASCUAL, Virginia (8)**	**ESP**
58. GARCIA, Paula	ESP
59. SCHEEPERS, Chanelle	RSA
60. BLACK, Cara	ZIM
61. VESNINA, Elena	RUS
62. KONDRATIEVA, Maria	RUS
63. ERAKOVIC, Marina	NZL
64. **ANI, Maret (20)**	**EST**
65. **GAGLIARDI, Emmanuelle (9)**	**SUI**
66. DZEHALEVICH, Ekaterina	BLR
67. FUDA, Ryoko	JPN
68. KANEPI, Kaia	EST
69. CHUANG, Chia-Jung	TPE
70. TAO, Sunitha	USA
71. BRENGLE, Madison (WC)	USA
72. **KUTUZOVA, Viktoriya (25)**	**UKR**
73. **PANOVA, Tatiana (10)**	**RUS**
74. GAJDOSOVA, Jarmila	SVK
75. KORYTTSEVA, Mariya	UKR
76. BRADLEY, Megan (WC)	USA
77. PARMENTIER, Pauline (WC)	FRA
78. KOPS-JONES, Raquel (WC)	USA
79. DITTY, Julie	USA
80. **VOSKOBOEVA, Galina (24)**	**RUS**
81. **YAKIMOVA, Anastasiya (11)**	**BLR**
82. BRATCHIKOVA, Nina	RUS
83. POUTCHEK, Tatiana	BLR
84. FLIPKENS, Kirsten	BEL
85. OSTERLOH, Lilia	USA
86. ASHLEY, Teryn	USA
87. JUGIC-SALKIC, Mervana	BIH
88. **SALERNI, Maria Emilia (21)**	**ARG**
89. **DOMINIKOVIC, Evie (12)**	**AUS**
90. TALAJA, Silvija	CRO
91. CASTELLVI, Vilmarie	PUR
92. PICHET, Virginie	FRA
93. OKAMOTO, Seiko	JPN
94. OZEGOVIC, Nika	CRO
95. HROZENSKA, Stanislava	SVK
96. **MULLER, Martina (28)**	**GER**
97. **OBZILER, Tzipora (13)**	**ISR**
98. GRANDIN, Natalie	RSA
99. DUBOIS, Stephanie	CAN
100. MARTINEZ GRANADOS, C.	ESP
101. KREMER, Anne	LUX
102. MEZAK, Matea	CRO
103. COHEN, Julia (WC)	USA
104. **MEUSBURGER, Yvonne (26)**	**AUT**
105. **PELLETIER, Marie-Eve (14)**	**CAN**
106. SNYDER, Tara (WC)	USA
107. NOONI, Hanna	SWE
108. KURHAJCOVA, Lubomira	SVK
109. KLEINOVA, Sandra	CZE
110. ROLLE, Ahsha	USA
111. CHAN, Yung-Jan	TPE
112. **BALTACHA, Elena (27)**	**GBR**
113. **FORETZ, Stephanie (15)**	**FRA**
114. HRDINOVA, Eva	CZE
115. BONDARENKO, Kateryna	UKR
116. RUUTEL, Margit	EST
117. WOERLE, Kathrin	GER
118. SFAR, Selima	TUN
119. CALLENS, Els	BEL
120. **CZINK, Melinda (19)**	**HUN**
121. **LEPCHENKO, Varvara (16)**	**UZB**
122. KACHLIKOVA, Katarina	SVK
123. KING, Vania (WC)	USA
124. ABRAMOVIC, Ivana	CRO
125. NAGY, Kyra	HUN
126. NAGYOVA, Henrieta	SVK
127. YUAN, Meng	CHN
128. **GALLOVITS, Edina (30)**	**ROM**

First Round

Winner	Score
BAMMER	6-2, 3-6, 6-3
YAN	6-3, 6-3
MAKAROVA	6-2, 3-6, 6-4
UBEROI, S.	0-6, 7-5, 6-3
HOPKINS	6-2, 4-6, 6-2
UBEROI, N.	6-1, 6-1
KUTI-KIS	6-4, 6-2
LISJAK	7-6(3), 6-1
SANCHEZ LORENZO	3-6, 6-0, 6-3
SAVCHUK	6-2, 6-3
CANEPA	6-3, 6-2
LAINE	6-3, 6-1
PIRONKOVA	6-4, 6-4
DABEK	6-3, 5-7, 7-5
HRADECKA	6-3, 7-6(2)
ALVES	6-4, 6-2
ANTYPINA	6-4, 6-4
SUN	6-2, 6-0
PRUSOVA	6-4, 6-2
CERVANOVA	6-3, 6-1
SROMOVA	7-5, 6-3
HSIEH	6-1, 6-3
SEQUERA	3-6, 7-6(5), 7-5
NOCIAROVA	6-0, 6-2
KLOESEL	6-2, 5-7, 6-4
BACHMANN	6-0, 6-3
SCHAUL	5-7, 7-5, 7-6(6)
TU	6-4, 6-1
RUANO PASCUAL	6-2, 6-2
SCHEEPERS	3-6, 6-3, 6-2
VESNINA	2-6, 6-2, 6-4
ERAKOVIC	6-3, 6-2
GAGLIARDI	5-7, 6-3, 6-0
KANEPI	6-4, 6-4
RAO	4-6, 6-4, 6-1
KUTUZOVA	6-1, 6-2
PANOVA	6-4, 6-4
BRADLEY	7-5, 6-3
PARMENTIER	6-4, 6-4
VOSKOBOEVA	6-2, 6-7(3), 6-2
YAKIMOVA	6-4, 6-2
POUTCHEK	4-6, 6-3, 7-6(1)
OSTERLOH	6-1, 6-2
SALERNI	6-2, 7-6(7)
TALAJA	7-5, 7-6(5)
CASTELLVI	6-2, 6-4
OKAMOTO	7-5, 7-6(0)
MULLER	6-2, 6-4
GRANDIN	6-1, 6-4
DUBOIS	6-0, 6-1
KREMER	6-4, 6-1
MEUSBURGER	6-2, 6-4
SNYDER	6-3, 6-2
KURHAJCOVA	6-3, 6-2
ROLLE	6-2, 6-3
CHAN	6-1, 6-0
FORETZ	6-3, 6-2
BONDARENKO	6-0, 6-1
WOERLE	3-6, 6-1, 6-3
CALLENS	4-6, 6-1, 6-2
KACHLIKOVA	7-5, 6-7(1), 6-2
KING	6-2, 5-7, 6-0
NAGY	6-2, 4-6, 5-0 RET.
GALLOVITS	6-3, 1-6, 6-4

Second Round

Winner	Score
BAMMER	4-6, 6-4, 6-4
UBEROI, S.	7-5, 3-6, 6-4
HOPKINS	7-5, 5-7, 6-2
LISJAK	4-6, 6-1, 6-4
SANCHEZ LORENZO	4-6, 6-4, 7-6(3)
LAINE	7-6(6), 6-0
DABEK	6-3, 4-6, 6-2
ALVES	6-3, 6-2
SUN	6-2, 7-6(4)
CERVANOVA	4-6, 6-2, 6-0
HSIEH	4-6, 7-6(3), 6-1
SEQUERA	6-2, 5-7, 6-0
KLOESEL	7-5, 3-6, 6-0
SCHAUL	4-6, 6-2, 6-2
RUANO PASCUAL	6-2, 6-1
ERAKOVIC	6-2, 6-1
GAGLIARDI	6-4, 6-2
KUTUZOVA	6-1, 6-2
PANOVA	3-6, 6-0, 6-1
PARMENTIER	0-6, 7-6(5), 6-4
YAKIMOVA	6-4, 6-2
SALERNI	7-6(4), 7-6(3)
CASTELLVI	6-7(3), 6-3, 6-2
MULLER	6-4, 6-2
GRANDIN	6-0, 6-2
KREMER	7-6(5), 6-0
KURHAJCOVA	3-6, 6-2, 7-5
CHAN	6-2, 6-3
FORETZ	6-2, 7-6(5)
WOERLE	6-3, 6-1
KING	5-7, 6-3, 6-3
GALLOVITS	6-0, 7-6(5)

Final Round

Winner	Score
BAMMER	7-6(5), 6-2
LISJAK	6-3, 7-6(10)
LAINE	6-4, 6-4
DABEK	4-6, 6-2, 6-3
SUN	6-1, 6-2
HSIEH	7-5, 6-3
KLOESEL	6-4, 6-3
RUANO PASCUAL	7-5, 6-3
KUTUZOVA	6-4, 6-1
PARMENTIER	6-3, 1-6, 6-3
SALERNI	7-5, 6-2
MULLER	6-3, 1-6, 6-1
KREMER	4-6, 6-0, 6-2
CHAN	6-1, 6-4
FORETZ	6-3, 4-6, 6-4
KING	6-4, 6-7(1), 6-4

NO MORE MS. NICE GUY

When redemption hung in the balance, Kim Clijsters emerged as no longer the nicest, best player never to win a major

by Richard Pagliaro

KIM CLIJSTERS

POLO

Graceful falls in major matches were common climaxes for Kim Clijsters, who has teetered on the very edge of Grand Slam glory only to fall frustratingly short in four Grand Slam tournament finals. Tagged with the label of best player never to win a major that clung to her as tightly as a tattoo, Clijsters faced each setback with the characteristic class of a woman well aware there's much more to life than the outcome of a tennis match. By the end of the Saturday night U.S. Open prime-time showdown, she was again straddling a major precipice. Dangling dangerously on the ledge of loss once again, Clijsters struggled to maintain balance with 23,000 fans riveted by her precarious predicament.

Moments after capturing the first Grand Slam tournament crown of her career, in a 6-3, 6-1 comprehensive conquest of Mary Pierce, an ecstatic Clijsters tossed her racquet aside, sprinted to the corner of the court, scaled up the side wall with all the exuberance of a rock climber, balanced on a ledge and leaped into the embracing arms of her mother, Els, and coach, Marc Dehous, in the support box.

"As soon as I looked over to the them, I just wanted to hug them," Clijsters said. "I just decided to run up there."

Confronting life-altering events during the past year, including an injury that placed her career at break point and the heartbreak caused by the breakup of her engagement to Lleyton Hewitt, Clijsters failed to surpass the fourth round at Roland Garros or Wimbledon. However, she spent the summer climbing back toward the top in sweeping tournament titles in Stanford, Los Angeles and Toronto without dropping a set in those 13 matches to claim the U.S. Open Series title. By the day of the U.S. Open final, the fourth-seeded Clijsters carried a 36-1 hard court record and a tour-best six tournament titles into a clash of comeback competitors.

Persevering through disappointing

FILA

defeats, the 22-year-old Clijsters reached her desired destination by overcoming surgery on her left wrist in June 2004. The recovery sidelined her for nearly nine months, causing her ranking to plummet to No. 133 as recently as March. She reaped the rewards for her committed comeback by collecting the U.S. Open title trophy and a record champion's check of $2.2 million — the largest payday in women's sports history.

"There is a time and place for everything; maybe it wasn't my time yet in those Grand Slams," said Clijsters, who spent the 2004 U.S. Open with her wrist wrapped in a plaster cast while cheering for Hewitt in the same support box she leaped into on Saturday night. "Losing those Grand Slams definitely motivates you to work harder. There's been a lot of very boring weeks when I was injured, when I was in the plasters, trying to recover and doing all these crazy exercises. You have to have your family, your friends to help you, to push you, to go for it. Maybe that's why I'm sitting here now with this trophy next to me."

Seemingly shedding slivers of her sneaker soles with her speedy sprints, skids and splits, Clijsters combines the leg strength of a speed skater, the body control of a break dancer and the dogged determination of a bounty hunter pursuing every single ball as if it were a felt-disguised fugitive fleeing from justice meted out by her blue Babolat racquet. The quick-footed Clijsters seemed to shrink the largest court in the world to the size of a hopscotch board as her rapid retrievals compelled the 30-year-old Pierce to raise the risk level on her shots and play low percentage down-the-line drives from the very first game.

The first French woman to contest the U.S. Open final, the Montreal-born Pierce, who finished second in the U.S. Open series, dispatched former No. 1 players Justine Henin-Hardenne and Amelie Mauresmo in straight sets to reach the final four. Surrendering a set for the first time in the tournament to Elena Dementieva, Pierce, whose ritualistic pre-point primping resembles a third base coaching issuing a hit-and-run sign, took a controversial 12-minute injury timeout for massage treatment of her back and thigh that altered the momentum of the match. When play resumed, a revived Pierce recovered; Dementieva did not. Pounding away with renewed aggression, Pierce pummeled the sixth-seeded Russian in the final two sets for a 3-6, 6-2, 6-2 victory that vaulted her into her first Flushing Meadows final.

"You can change the game around by winning an unbelievable point or by changing the rhythm," said Dementieva. "That's the fair point. But by taking like a 12-minute time out, I don't think it was fair play. She could do it by the rules. And she did it. If that's the only way she can beat me, it's up to her."

The 12th-seeded Pierce rebounded from her lopsided loss to Henin-

Hardenne in the Roland Garros final by producing a 12-match hard-court winning streak. The ominous shadow of her domineering dad, Jim Pierce, has been diminished as Mary calls her own shots, enjoying a productive partnership with her brother and coach, David, and former coach Nick Bollettieri back in her box as a coaching consultant.

A sleeker, stronger Pierce was playing perhaps the best tennis of her career, but her inspired run was halted by Clijsters, who competed with the conviction of a woman who won by refusing to accept any point was a lost cause. Pierce served to start the match and took a 30-0 lead before Clijsters, sliding into successive speedy splits to save would-be winners, battled back to break serve when Pierce bashed consecutive backhands into the net. Clijsters quickly consolidated the break to take a 2-0 lead. In the space of that sequence, Pierce sensed she was in trouble, even at that early stage.

"I knew in the very first game, when she came back to 30-all, I knew it was going to be a tough, a very tough match," said Pierce, who has realized her own career resurrection in rebounding from a low point of No. 295 in April of 2002. "She's got a different style than any girls I've played against this week or these two weeks. She's a great girl. She's a champion."

The blonde Belgian began the U.S. Open contemplating retirement and concluded it crafting a compelling comeback that resulted in rewarding redemption.

Days before the start of the Flushing Meadows fortnight, Clijsters declared her desire to retire from the rigors of the pro circuit within three years.

"I see myself stopping in 2007 or early 2008," Clijsters said. "My body already has a lot of problems. It might sound odd, but it all becomes a bit heavy on me: the tournaments, the traveling. I can't see me doing this for more than another two or three years. I don't think my body can handle this lifestyle for that much longer."

It's a lifestyle that sapped the strength of several of the sport's stars, including Henin-Hardenne, Lindsay Davenport, Maria Sharapova, Serena Williams and Venus Williams, who were each sidelined with injury or illness for sustained stretches of the summer hard court season while another former top-ranked champion and perennially-popular presence in New York — Jennifer Capriati — did not strike a shot all season in continuing recovery from shoulder surgery. Fluctuating physical states of the contenders were reflected in results. For the second straight season, four different women won the four majors.

The demands of the Sony Ericsson WTA Tour schedule make it a convenient scapegoat, but the truth is that some of the top players simply did not schedule smartly or show up in shape to contend for the season's final Slam. Serena started the season with a stirring surge to the Australian Open title and Venus silenced skeptics by winning Wimbledon in a dramatic duel with Davenport, but both sisters were more visible as Reality TV stars than tennis players during the U.S. Open Series. Serena still owns the skills to rule the tennis world, but trying to win the Open with just one hard court match as preparation is as wise as trying to swim the Hudson River while trapped in a straightjacket.

In contrast, some tour veterans showed signs of staying power: 32-year-old Lisa Raymond and Australian Samantha Stosur defeated Dementieva and Flavia Pennetta to win the women's doubles title; 32-year-old Amy Frazier competed in her 19th consecutive Open and 67th major overall; Daniela Hantuchova partnered Mahesh Bhupathi to win the mixed doubles title

MARY PIERCE

and complete a career mixed doubles Grand Slam; and, finally, there is Martina Navratilova, reaching the women's doubles semifinals with partner Anna-Lena Groenfeld and the mixed doubles quarters with Leander Paes.

Clijsters used her time off from tennis to strengthen her body — her superior stamina was a key component in consecutive three-set victories — and to stabilize her forehand, which has been her weaker wing, but became the focus of her training when she was restricted from hitting her two-handed backhand for several months.

"I think all that has definitely made me a physically stronger person," said Clijsters, who was inspired by Andre Agassi, another former No. 1 who lost his first three major finals, underwent wrist surgery and plummeted past No. 130 in the rankings before rededicating himself to tennis.

While Pierce and Clijsters were committed, concentration cracks were apparent in some former champions.

The top-ranked Davenport played oddly apathetic tennis in the opening set of her quarterfinal and spent much of the match fighting herself and a determined Dementieva. Ultimately, Davenport could not overcome either opponent or an unsightly 56 unforced errors in bowing 6-1, 3-6, 7-6 (6).

Facing Dementieva's slice serve is a bit like playing Russian Roulette with a pop gun: it's not strong enough to be fatal, but it can be unsettling, particularly when she follows up a soft serve with her cannon-fired forehand. Dementieva showed grit and guts in withstanding 12 double faults and saving a match point at 5-6 in the tie-break with a ferocious forehand that singed the sideline.

A disconsolate Davenport was forced to face her latest Grand Slam disappointment. She held a one-set lead before bowing to Serena in the Australian Open final in January and was one point from winning Wimbledon before succumbing to Venus in

JUSTINE HENIN-HARDENNE (l) AND MARY PIERCE (r)

ental
ines

July, and she continues to struggle in closing out major matches.

"It sucks," said Davenport, five years removed from her last major title. "I was trying. But I still could have pulled that match out playing the way I did, and sometimes you've got to be able to do that in Grand Slams."

A year after she became the lowest-seeded woman to claim the U.S. Open in the Open Era, Svetlana Kuzentsova made history again as the first defending women's champion to fall in the first round, imploding in a scatter-shot performance of 45 unforced errors when she succumbed to fellow Russian Ekaterina Bychkova, 6-3, 6-2.

"Now, no one will disturb me about this [defending the title]," a clear-eyed Kuznetsova said. "I tried my best; it wasn't my day. What do I do? Kill myself? No, I don't. Just try to take positive things out of this and maybe I'll try to learn."

The learning curve took an accelerated course for talented teenagers Nicole Vaidisova and Sania Mirza, who both registered career-best performances by reaching the fourth round, the same stage at which the Williams sisters met in their first pre-quarterfinal Grand Slam clash since their first match in the second round of the 1998 Australian Open.

Minutes into her opening-round match, a section of one of the $40,000 Erica Courtney-designed "Dream Catcher" diamond and platinum earrings hanging from Serena's ears like small chandeliers fell to the court, scattering a few diamonds behind the baseline as Williams bent over to retrieve them.

Only Serena could turn Arthur Ashe Stadium into a temporary Tennis Diamond District, but she couldn't pick up the pieces of her game, dulled to the status of cubic zirconia by questionable conditioning. Since she stumbled out of Wimbledon in the third round, eighth-seeded Serena had played just four matches prior to renewing this sibling rivalry on court.

Erratic conditions and competitors did not inspire high drama or high-quality tennis as swirling winds and patchy play from the sisters combined to create a match Venus and Serena both characterized as "bizarre."

Still, Serena's competitive spirit was evident as she rallied from a 3-5 first-set deficit and earned a set point in the 12th game of that set, but Venus won seven of the final nine games to even the sisters' head-to-head series at 7-7.

"I don't think I played my best today at all," Serena said. "I don't think Venus did either. I told her just how horrible we played. I said, 'You played terrible.' She was like 'I know.'"

The 10th-seeded Venus had won six of nine meetings with Clijsters prior to their quarterfinal collision, and when the two-time Open champion served with a 6-4, 4-2 lead Clijsters was down and nearly out of the tournament. But a weary Williams was unable to sustain her earlier fast pace of play and could not close an opponent playing tenacious tennis that still troubled her 10 minutes after the match was over.

As gracious as she was in winning Wimbledon to restore her own championship status, Williams was equally ungracious in dissing Clijsters' comeback.

"She started playing really bad, and it totally threw me off," Williams said. "She started hitting these really weird shots and short balls. It threw my game off. Next thing I knew, I was playing as bad as she was, and she was able to recover."

Defending with determination, Clijsters simply wore Venus out in rallying for a 4-6, 7-5, 6-1 victory.

"I wasn't really thinking about the score; I just tried to keep fighting and keep running for each ball," Clijsters said.

MARIA SHARAPOVA

It was precisely the game plan she used to stave off a stubborn, shrieking Sharapova, converting her sixth match point to post a 6-2, 6-7 (4), 6-3 semifinal victory. Glancing up to her father, Yuri, for constant guidance in the face of a second-set deficit, the top-seeded Sharapova battled back to save five match points, seizing the second set and the momentum. At that point, it seemed entirely possibly the ghosts of Grand Slam failures past would haunt Clijsters, but even one of tennis's hardest hitters could not detour Clijsters' comeback run. Playing with passion and purpose, Clijsters won 16 of the first 22 points to race out to a 4-0 lead. Sharapova strikes the ball as well as any woman on tour, but she's still growing into her body, plays at one predictably powerful pace and cannot match the movement of Clijsters, Henin-Hardenne or the Williams sisters.

With the exception of her screaming shrieks that turn every point into an exclamation point, the top-seeded Sharapova quietly streaked through the draw, dropping just 12 games en route to the quarterfinals, where she unleashed vicious crosscourt forehands in the final set to subdue Nadia Petrova, 7-5, 4-6, 6-4. Though the 2004 Wimbledon winner has reached the semifinals in nine of the 12 tournaments she has played this year, Clijsters exposed the deficiencies in the 18-year-old's game. The player behind the brand can still struggle against speedy opponents adept at altering spins; she is not comfortable closing points at net; she does not hit as well on the run as several players in the Top 10; and she could not combat Clijsters' strength in the final set of their semi, conceding she "ran out of gas."

In the aftermath of that semifinal, Clijsters embraced her mother in a heartfelt hug in the hallway beneath the stadium.

The Clijsters family is a close one whose members leaned on each other for support when Els Clijsters underwent a liver transplant in March of 1999. The fact

prince

ELENA DEMENTIEVA

LINDSAY DAVENPORT

org

that mother and daughter are so close has heightened Kim's desire to have children while she's still young and build a bond similar to the one she has shared with her own mother, who is sometimes mistaken for her sister when the pair are approached in public.

It was Clijsters' mother who introduced her to her current boyfriend, former Villanova University basketball player Brian Lynch, who now plays professionally in Bree, Belgium. The couple both own bulldogs, met over a doggie date and noticed an instant attraction: Lynch's bulldog, who had yet to be fixed, was all over Clijsters' dog. Prior to the start of the North American summer season, Clijsters spent 10 days with Lynch and his family at the Jersey Shore, training and visiting the state's largest amusement park together before embarking on her own Great Adventure that would conclude on the other side of the George Washington Bridge.

A year earlier, her left wrist wrapped in a plaster cast, Clijsters would have struggled to pick up a box of Kleenex in one hand. But by the end of this year's event, she was hoisting the shiny silver U.S. Open trophy, seeing herself in its reflection and reflecting on what she saw.

"People are saying, 'You've matured.' I don't think it's matured. I think I just got to know myself a lot better," Clijsters said. "When I got injured, I was home for longer than I've ever been home. I was never home for more than two weeks before that. Now all of a sudden I was home three, four months in a row. And now I have the perfect balance between life on the road and life off the road. That's something that I was looking for for a long time: to have the balance."

On a Saturday night in New York with her toes tap dancing on the edge of the stadium wall, Clijsters successfully straddled personal and professional challenges to find that sense of stability she has long sought.

Rbk

AMELIE MAURESMO

NADIA PETROVA

VENUS WILLIAMS

JUSTINE HENIN-HARDENNE

Wilson

SERENA WILLIAMS

SERENA WILLIAMS (l) AND VENUS WILLIAMS (r))

SERENA WILLIAMS

SERENA WILLIAMS

SANIA MIRZA

SANIA MIRZA

GVK

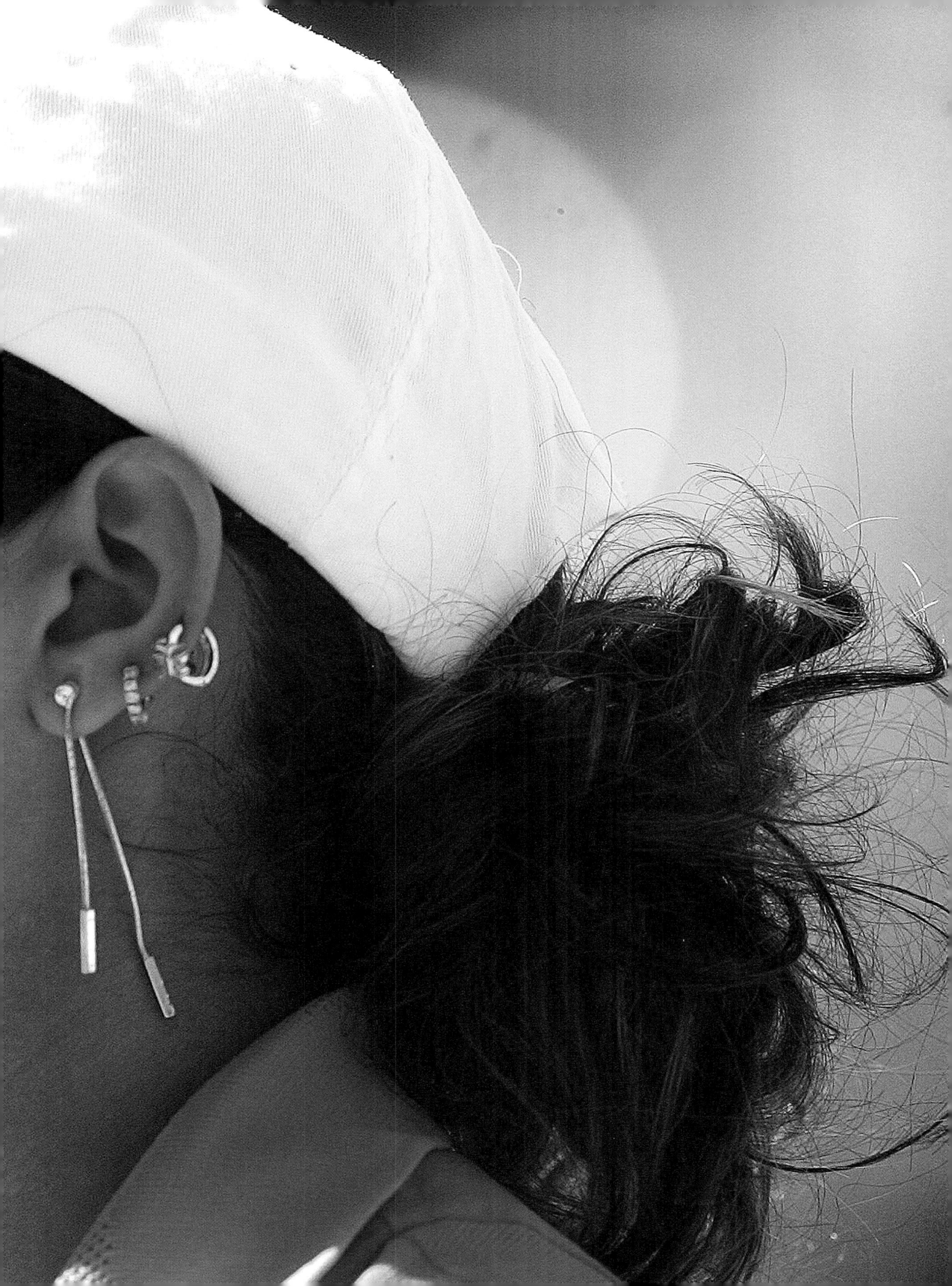

PATTY SCHNYDER

LIQUIDMETAL
adidas

NICOLE VAIDISOVA

RbK

AI SUGIYAMA

ANNA-LENA GROENEFELD

FRANCESCA SCHIAVONE

ANASTASIA MYSKINA

KIM CLIJSTERS

U.S. OPEN WOMEN'S SINGLES DRAW

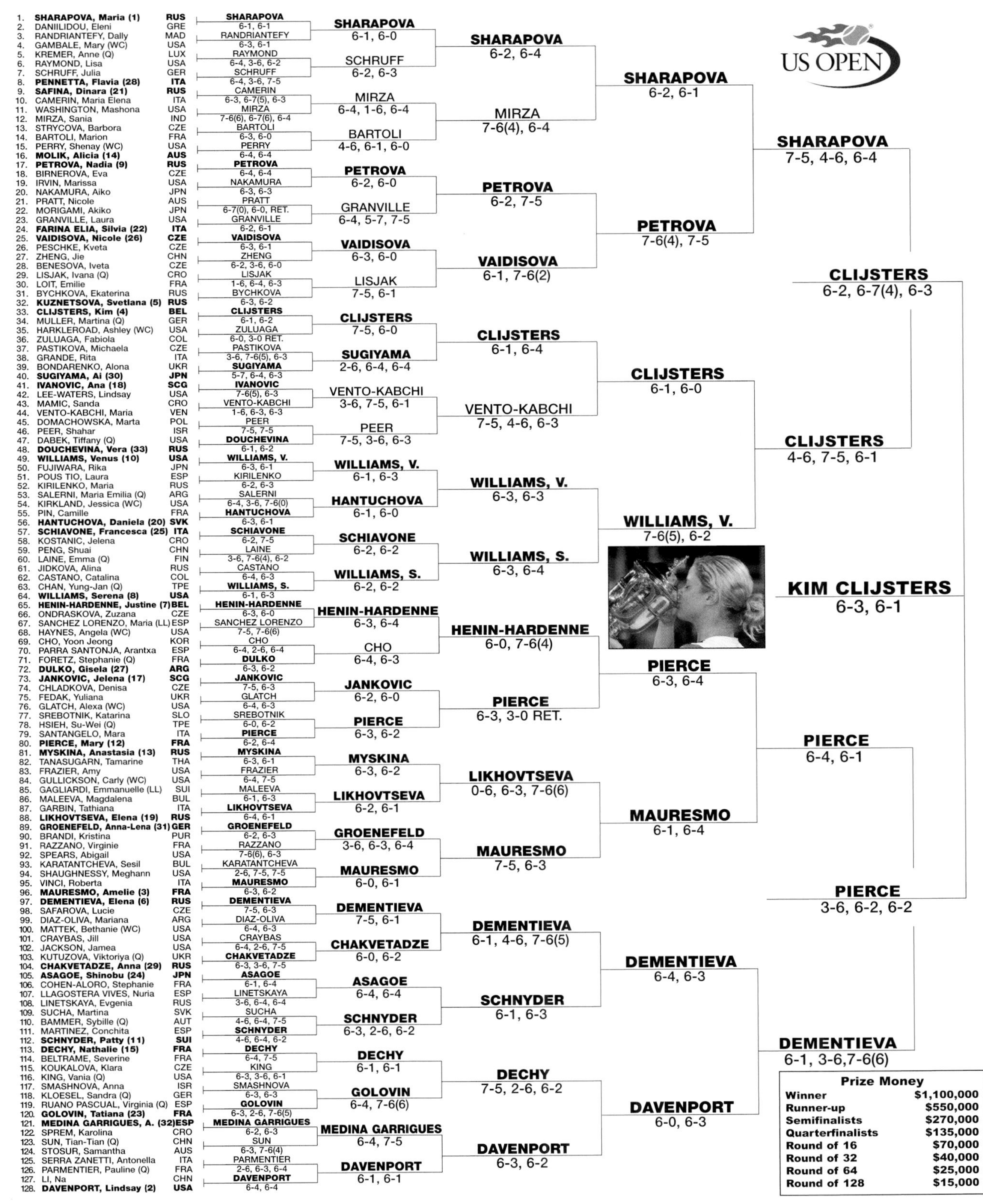

1.	**SHARAPOVA, Maria (1)**	**RUS**
2.	DANIILIDOU, Eleni	GRE
3.	RANDRIANTEFY, Dally	MAD
4.	GAMBALE, Mary (WC)	USA
5.	KREMER, Anne (Q)	LUX
6.	RAYMOND, Lisa	USA
7.	SCHRUFF, Julia	GER
8.	**PENNETTA, Flavia (28)**	**ITA**
9.	**SAFINA, Dinara (21)**	**RUS**
10.	CAMERIN, Maria Elena	ITA
11.	WASHINGTON, Mashona	USA
12.	MIRZA, Sania	IND
13.	STRYCOVA, Barbora	CZE
14.	BARTOLI, Marion	FRA
15.	PERRY, Shenay (WC)	USA
16.	**MOLIK, Alicia (14)**	**AUS**
17.	**PETROVA, Nadia (9)**	**RUS**
18.	BIRNEROVA, Eva	CZE
19.	IRVIN, Marissa	USA
20.	NAKAMURA, Aiko	JPN
21.	PRATT, Nicole	AUS
22.	MORIGAMI, Akiko	JPN
23.	GRANVILLE, Laura	USA
24.	**FARINA ELIA, Silvia (22)**	**ITA**
25.	**VAIDISOVA, Nicole (26)**	**CZE**
26.	PESCHKE, Kveta	CZE
27.	ZHENG, Jie	CHN
28.	BENESOVA, Iveta	CZE
29.	LISJAK, Ivana (Q)	CRO
30.	LOIT, Emilie	FRA
31.	BYCHKOVA, Ekaterina	RUS
32.	**KUZNETSOVA, Svetlana (5)**	**RUS**
33.	**CLIJSTERS, Kim (4)**	**BEL**
34.	MULLER, Martina (Q)	GER
35.	HARKLEROAD, Ashley (WC)	USA
36.	ZULUAGA, Fabiola	COL
37.	PASTIKOVA, Michaela	CZE
38.	GRANDE, Rita	ITA
39.	BONDARENKO, Alona	UKR
40.	**SUGIYAMA, Ai (30)**	**JPN**
41.	**IVANOVIC, Ana (18)**	**SCG**
42.	LEE-WATERS, Lindsay	USA
43.	MAMIC, Sanda	CRO
44.	VENTO-KABCHI, Maria	VEN
45.	DOMACHOWSKA, Marta	POL
46.	PEER, Shahar	ISR
47.	DABEK, Tiffany (Q)	USA
48.	**DOUCHEVINA, Vera (33)**	**RUS**
49.	**WILLIAMS, Venus (10)**	**USA**
50.	FUJIWARA, Rika	JPN
51.	POUS TIO, Laura	ESP
52.	KIRILENKO, Maria	RUS
53.	SALERNI, Maria Emilia (Q)	ARG
54.	KIRKLAND, Jessica (WC)	USA
55.	PIN, Camille	FRA
56.	**HANTUCHOVA, Daniela (20)**	**SVK**
57.	**SCHIAVONE, Francesca (25)**	**ITA**
58.	KOSTANIC, Jelena	CRO
59.	PENG, Shuai	CHN
60.	LAINE, Emma (Q)	FIN
61.	JIDKOVA, Alina	RUS
62.	CASTANO, Catalina	COL
63.	CHAN, Yung-Jan (Q)	TPE
64.	**WILLIAMS, Serena (8)**	**USA**
65.	**HENIN-HARDENNE, Justine (7)**	**BEL**
66.	ONDRASKOVA, Zuzana	CZE
67.	SANCHEZ LORENZO, Maria (LL)	ESP
68.	HAYNES, Angela (WC)	USA
69.	CHO, Yoon Jeong	KOR
70.	PARRA SANTONJA, Arantxa	ESP
71.	FORETZ, Stephanie (Q)	FRA
72.	**DULKO, Gisela (27)**	**ARG**
73.	**JANKOVIC, Jelena (17)**	**SCG**
74.	CHLADKOVA, Denisa	CZE
75.	FEDAK, Yuliana	UKR
76.	GLATCH, Alexa (WC)	USA
77.	SREBOTNIK, Katarina	SLO
78.	HSIEH, Su-Wei (Q)	TPE
79.	SANTANGELO, Mara	ITA
80.	**PIERCE, Mary (12)**	**FRA**
81.	**MYSKINA, Anastasia (13)**	**RUS**
82.	TANASUGARN, Tamarine	THA
83.	FRAZIER, Amy	USA
84.	GULLICKSON, Carly (WC)	USA
85.	GAGLIARDI, Emmanuelle (LL)	SUI
86.	MALEEVA, Magdalena	BUL
87.	GARBIN, Tathiana	ITA
88.	**LIKHOVTSEVA, Elena (19)**	**RUS**
89.	**GROENEFELD, Anna-Lena (31)**	**GER**
90.	BRANDI, Kristina	PUR
91.	RAZZANO, Virginie	FRA
92.	SPEARS, Abigail	USA
93.	KARATANTCHEVA, Sesil	BUL
94.	SHAUGHNESSY, Meghann	USA
95.	VINCI, Roberta	ITA
96.	**MAURESMO, Amelie (3)**	**FRA**
97.	**DEMENTIEVA, Elena (6)**	**RUS**
98.	SAFAROVA, Lucie	CZE
99.	DIAZ-OLIVA, Mariana	ARG
100.	MATTEK, Bethanie (WC)	USA
101.	CRAYBAS, Jill	USA
102.	JACKSON, Jamea	USA
103.	KUTUZOVA, Viktoriya (Q)	UKR
104.	**CHAKVETADZE, Anna (29)**	**RUS**
105.	**ASAGOE, Shinobu (24)**	**JPN**
106.	COHEN-ALORO, Stephanie	FRA
107.	LLAGOSTERA VIVES, Nuria	ESP
108.	LINETSKAYA, Evgenia	RUS
109.	SUCHA, Martina	SVK
110.	BAMMER, Sybille (Q)	AUT
111.	MARTINEZ, Conchita	ESP
112.	**SCHNYDER, Patty (11)**	**SUI**
113.	**DECHY, Nathalie (15)**	**FRA**
114.	BELTRAME, Severine	FRA
115.	KOUKALOVA, Klara	CZE
116.	KING, Vania (Q)	USA
117.	SMASHNOVA, Anna	ISR
118.	KLOESEL, Sandra (Q)	GER
119.	RUANO PASCUAL, Virginia (Q)	ESP
120.	**GOLOVIN, Tatiana (23)**	**FRA**
121.	**MEDINA GARRIGUES, A. (32)**	**ESP**
122.	SPREM, Karolina	CRO
123.	SUN, Tian-Tian (Q)	CHN
124.	STOSUR, Samantha	AUS
125.	SERRA ZANETTI, Antonella	ITA
126.	PARMENTIER, Pauline (Q)	FRA
127.	LI, Na	CHN
128.	**DAVENPORT, Lindsay (2)**	**USA**

SHARAPOVA 6-1, 6-1
RANDRIANTEFY 6-3, 6-1
RAYMOND 6-4, 3-6, 6-2
SCHRUFF 6-4, 3-6, 7-5
CAMERIN 6-3, 6-7(5), 6-3
MIRZA 7-6(6), 6-7(6), 6-4
BARTOLI 6-3, 6-0
PERRY 6-4, 6-4
PETROVA 6-4, 6-4
NAKAMURA 6-3, 6-3
PRATT 6-7(0), 6-0, RET.
GRANVILLE 6-2, 6-1
VAIDISOVA 6-3, 6-1
ZHENG 6-2, 3-6, 6-0
LISJAK 1-6, 6-4, 6-3
BYCHKOVA 6-3, 6-2
CLIJSTERS 6-1, 6-2
ZULUAGA 6-0, 3-0 RET.
PASTIKOVA 3-6, 7-6(5), 6-3
SUGIYAMA 5-7, 6-4, 6-3
IVANOVIC 7-6(5), 6-3
VENTO-KABCHI 1-6, 6-3, 6-3
PEER 7-5, 7-5
DOUCHEVINA 6-1, 6-2
WILLIAMS, V. 6-3, 6-1
KIRILENKO 6-2, 6-3
SALERNI 6-4, 3-6, 7-6(0)
HANTUCHOVA 6-3, 6-1
SCHIAVONE 6-2, 7-5
LAINE 3-6, 7-6(4), 6-2
CASTANO 6-4, 6-3
WILLIAMS, S. 6-1, 6-3
HENIN-HARDENNE 6-3, 6-0
SANCHEZ LORENZO 7-5, 7-6(6)
CHO 6-4, 2-6, 6-4
DULKO 6-3, 6-2
JANKOVIC 7-5, 6-3
GLATCH 6-4, 6-3
SREBOTNIK 6-0, 6-2
PIERCE 6-2, 6-4
MYSKINA 6-3, 6-1
FRAZIER 6-4, 7-5
MALEEVA 6-1, 6-3
LIKHOVTSEVA 6-4, 6-1
GROENEFELD 6-2, 6-3
RAZZANO 7-6(6), 6-3
KARATANTCHEVA 2-6, 7-5, 7-5
MAURESMO 6-3, 6-2
DEMENTIEVA 7-5, 6-3
DIAZ-OLIVA 6-4, 6-3
CRAYBAS 6-4, 2-6, 7-5
CHAKVETADZE 6-3, 3-6, 7-5
ASAGOE 6-1, 6-4
LINETSKAYA 3-6, 6-4, 6-4
SUCHA 4-6, 6-4, 7-5
SCHNYDER 4-6, 6-4, 6-2
DECHY 6-4, 7-5
KING 6-3, 3-6, 6-1
SMASHNOVA 6-3, 6-3
GOLOVIN 6-3, 2-6, 7-6(5)
MEDINA GARRIGUES 6-2, 6-3
SUN 6-3, 7-6(4)
PARMENTIER 2-6, 6-3, 6-4
DAVENPORT 6-4, 6-4

SHARAPOVA 6-1, 6-0
SCHRUFF 6-2, 6-3
MIRZA 6-4, 1-6, 6-4
BARTOLI 4-6, 6-1, 6-0
PETROVA 6-2, 6-0
GRANVILLE 6-4, 5-7, 7-5
VAIDISOVA 6-3, 6-0
LISJAK 7-5, 6-1
CLIJSTERS 7-5, 6-0
SUGIYAMA 2-6, 6-4, 6-4
VENTO-KABCHI 3-6, 7-5, 6-1
PEER 7-5, 3-6, 6-3
WILLIAMS, V. 6-1, 6-3
HANTUCHOVA 6-1, 6-0
SCHIAVONE 6-2, 6-2
WILLIAMS, S. 6-2, 6-2
HENIN-HARDENNE 6-3, 6-4
CHO 6-4, 6-3
JANKOVIC 6-2, 6-0
PIERCE 6-3, 6-2
MYSKINA 6-3, 6-2
LIKHOVTSEVA 6-2, 6-1
GROENEFELD 3-6, 6-3, 6-4
MAURESMO 6-0, 6-1
DEMENTIEVA 7-5, 6-1
CHAKVETADZE 6-0, 6-2
ASAGOE 6-4, 6-4
SCHNYDER 6-3, 2-6, 6-2
DECHY 6-1, 6-1
GOLOVIN 6-4, 7-6(6)
MEDINA GARRIGUES 6-4, 7-5
DAVENPORT 6-1, 6-1

SHARAPOVA 6-2, 6-4
MIRZA 7-6(4), 6-4
PETROVA 6-2, 7-5
VAIDISOVA 6-1, 7-6(2)
CLIJSTERS 6-1, 6-4
VENTO-KABCHI 7-5, 4-6, 6-3
WILLIAMS, V. 6-3, 6-3
WILLIAMS, S. 6-3, 6-4
HENIN-HARDENNE 6-0, 7-6(4)
PIERCE 6-3, 3-0 RET.
LIKHOVTSEVA 0-6, 6-3, 7-6(6)
MAURESMO 7-5, 6-3
DEMENTIEVA 6-1, 4-6, 7-6(5)
SCHNYDER 6-1, 6-3
DECHY 7-5, 2-6, 6-2
DAVENPORT 6-3, 6-2

SHARAPOVA 6-2, 6-1
PETROVA 7-6(4), 7-5
CLIJSTERS 6-1, 6-0
WILLIAMS, V. 7-6(5), 6-2
PIERCE 6-3, 6-4
MAURESMO 6-1, 6-4
DEMENTIEVA 6-4, 6-3
DAVENPORT 6-0, 6-3

SHARAPOVA 7-5, 4-6, 6-4
CLIJSTERS 4-6, 7-5, 6-1
PIERCE 6-4, 6-1
DEMENTIEVA 6-1, 3-6,7-6(6)

CLIJSTERS 6-2, 6-7(4), 6-3
PIERCE 3-6, 6-2, 6-2

KIM CLIJSTERS 6-3, 6-1

Prize Money	
Winner	**$1,100,000**
Runner-up	**$550,000**
Semifinalists	**$270,000**
Quarterfinalists	**$135,000**
Round of 16	**$70,000**
Round of 32	**$40,000**
Round of 64	**$25,000**
Round of 128	**$15,000**

LISA RAYMOND (l) AND SAMANTHA STOSUR (r)

U.S. OPEN WOMEN'S DOUBLES

PRIZE MONEY			
Winner	$400,000	Quarterfinalists	$50,000
Finalist	$200,000	Round of 16	$25,000
Semifinalists	$100,000	Round of 32	$15,000
		Round of 64	$10,000

BLACK, C. (ZIM)/STUBBS, R. (AUS) (1)
MCSHEA, L. (AUS)/SPEARS, A. (USA)
GRANVILLE, L./GULLICKSON, C. (USA)
CRAYBAS, J./TU, M. (USA)
BRANDI, K. (PUR)/DHENIN, C. (FRA)
RANDRIANTEFY, D. (MAD)/SMASHNOVA, A. (ISR)
FUJIWARA, R. (JPN)/LI, N. (CHN)
HUSAROVA, J. (SVK)/SCHIAVONE, F. (ITA) (15)
ASAGOE, S. (JPN)/SREBOTNIK, K. (SLO) (10)
HOPKINS, J./WASHINGTON, M. (USA)
HAYNES, A./MATTEK, B. (USA) (WC)
LIKHOVTSEVA, E. (RUS)/MALEEVA, M. (BUL)
DOUCHEVINA, V. (RUS)/PEER, S. (ISR)
BARTOLI, M. (FRA)/SEQUERA, M. (VEN)
DANIILIDOU, E. (GRE)/RUSSELL, J. (USA)
RAYMOND, L. (USA)/STOSUR, S. (AUS) (6)
MARTINEZ, C./RUANO PASCUAL, V. (ESP) (3)
GRANDE, R. (ITA)/TANASUGARN, T. (THA)
KOSTANIC, J./MAMIC, S. (CRO)
COHEN-ALORO, S. (FRA)/SFAR, S. (TUN)
ONDRASKOVA, Z (CZE)/SUCHA, M. (SVK)
CHLADKOVA, D. (CZE)/RAZZANO, V. (FRA)
BENESOVA, I. (CZE)/BEYGELZIMER, Y (UKR)
DULKO, G. (ARG)/KIRILENKO, M. (RUS) (16)
MEDINA GARRIGUES, A. (ESP)/SAFINA, D. (RUS) (9)
YAN, Z./ZHENG, J. (CHN)
CHUANG, C.J. (TPE)/MORIGAMI, A. (JPN)
IRVIN, M./JACKSON, J. (USA) (WC)
FRAZIER, A. (USA)/JIDKOVA, A. (RUS)
FORETZ, S. (FRA)/VAIDISOVA, N. (CZE)
GLATCH, A./KING, V. (USA) (WC)
HANTUCHOVA, D. (SVK)/SUGIYAMA, A. (JPN) (5)
MORARIU, C. (USA)/SCHNYDER, P. (SUI) (8)
KOUKALOVA, K./SAFAROVA, L. (CZE)
BRADLEY, M./MILLER, K. (USA) (WC)
CASTANO, C. (COL)/POUS TIO, L. (ESP)
JUGIC-SALKIC, M. (BIH)/PASTIKOVA, M. (CZE)
ASHLEY, T./KIRKLAND, J. (USA) (WC)
MIRZA, S. (IND)/STEWART, B. (AUS)
LOIT, E. (FRA)/PRATT, N. (AUS) (11)
DEMENTIEVA, E. (RUS)/PENNETTA, F. (ITA) (14)
CHAKVETADZE, A. (RUS)/GOLOVIN, T. (FRA)
RODRIGUEZ, R.M.A. (ESP)/DIAZ-OLIVA, M. (ARG)
MARRERO, M. (ESP)/SERRA ZANETTI, A. (ITA)
JANKOVIC, J. (SCG)/KIRZAN, T. (SLO)
DEKMEIJERE, L. (LAT)/KARATANTCHEVA, S. (BUL)
SALERNI, M.E. (ARG)/VENTO-KABCHI, M. (VEN)
PETROVA, N. (RUS)/SHAUGHNESSY, M. (USA) (4)
GROENEFELD, A.L. (GER)/NAVRATILOVA, M. (USA) (7)
HARKLEROAD, A./LEE-WATERS, L. (USA) (WC)
ROLIE, A./UBEROIT, N. (USA) (WC)
CALLENS, E. (BEL)/SANTANGELO, M. (ITA)
DOMACHOWSKA, M. (POL)/TALAJA, S. (CRO)
LEE, J. (TPE)/PENG, S. (CHN)
GAGLIARDI, E. (SUI)/WEINGARTNER, M. (GER)
LI, T./SUN, T. (CHN) (12)
PESCHKE, K./STRYCOVA, B. (CZE) (13)
CAMERIN, M.E./GARBIN, T. (ITA)
FARINA ELIA, S./VINCI, R. (ITA)
MIYAGI, N. (JPN)/MYSKINA, A. (RUS)
BIRNEROVA, E. (CZE)/VINC, A. (ROM)
DOMINGUEZ LINO, L./LLAGOSTERA VIVES, N. (ESP)
LINETSKAYA, E./VOSKOBOEVA, G. (RUS)
KUZNETSOVA, S. (RUS)/MOLIK, A. (AUS) (2)

BLACK/STUBBS 6-1, 6-3
CRAYBAS/TU 6-3, 6-4
RANDRIANTEFY/SMASHNOVA 7-5, 6-2
FUJIWARA/LI 7-6(5), 6-3
ASAGOE/SREBOTNIK 6-0, 6-1
LIKHOVTSEVA/MALEEVA 6-2, 4-6, 6-4
DOUCHEVINA/PEER 7-5, 5-7, 6-4
RAYMOND/STOSUR 6-2, 6-3
MARTINEZ/RUANO PASCUAL 6-3, 7-5
COHEN-ALORO/SFAR 6-7(10), 6-3, 6-3
CHLADKOVA/RAZZANO 6-3, 6-4
DULKO/KIRILENKO 6-4, 6-7(3), 6-1
YAN/ZHENG 6-2, 6-3
CHUANG/MORIGAMI 6-4, 6-3
FRAZIER/JIDKOVA 7-5, 4-6, 7-6(4)
HANTUCHOVA/SUGIYAMA 7-5, 6-0
MORARIU/SCHNYDER 7-5, 6-2
BRADLEY/MILLER 6-4, 6-2
JUGIC-SALKIC/PASTIKOVA 6-4, 6-3
LOIT/PRATT 6-2, 6-4
DEMENTIEVA/PENNETTA 6-3, 6-2
MARRERO/SERRA ZANETTI 6-1, 6-4
JANKOVIC/KRIZAN 6-4, 5-7, 6-3
PETROVA/SHAUGHNESSY 6-3, 6-7(4), 7-5
GROENEFELD/NAVRATILOVA 6-2, 6-2
ROLLE/UBEROI 6-1, 2-6, 6-4
LEE/PENG 6-7(5), 6-4, 6-2
LI/SUN 2-6, 7-5, 6-0
CAMERIN/GARBIN 7-6(4), 7-5
FARINA ELIA/VINCI 3-6, 7-6(9), 6-2
BIRNEROVA/VANC 2-6, 6-3, 6-4
KUZNETSOVA/MOLIK 7-6(3), 6-2

BLACK/STUBBS
6-4, 6-3
FUJIWARA/LI
6-4, 7-5
ASAGOE/SREBOTNIK
6-2, 6-4
RAYMOND/STOSUR
6-3, 6-2
MARTINEZ/RUANO PASCUAL
7-5, 6-2
DULKO/KIRILENKO
6-2, 3-6, 6-4
YAN/ZHENG
6-3, 6-1
HANTUCHOVA/SUGIYAMA
2-6, 6-3, 6-3
MORARIU/SCHNYDER
6-2, 6-3
LOIT/PRATT
6-3, 6-2
DEMENTIEVA/PENNETTA
6-3, 6-4
PETROVA/SHAUGHNESSY
1-0 RET.
GROENEFELD/NAVRATILOVA
6-1, 6-0
LI/SUN
6-3, 6-4
FARINA ELIA/VINCI
6-2, 6-0
KUZNETSOVA/MOLIK
6-2, 6-2

BLACK/STUBBS
6-4, 7-6(3)
RAYMOND/STOSUR
6-1, 6-3
MARTINEZ/RUANO PASCUAL
4-6, 6-4, 6-2
YAN/ZHENG
6-3, 3-6, 7-5
MORARIU/SCHNYDER
6-3, 3-6, 6-4
DEMENTIEVA/PENNETTA
7-6(4), 6-3
GROENEFELD/NAVRATILOVA
2-6, 7-6(5), 6-1
KUZNETSOVA/MOLIK
6-3, 6-3

RAYMOND/STOSUR
5-7, 6-4, 6-4
MARTINEZ/RUANO PASCUAL
6-3, 6-4
DEMENTIEVA/PENNETTA
6-3, 3-6, 6-3
GROENEFELD/NAVRATILOVA
6-7(5), 7-5, 7-5

RAYMOND/STOSUR
7-5, 4-6, 7-6(2)
DEMENTIEVA/PENNETTA
6-2, 6-4

RAYMOND/STOSUR
6-2, 5-7, 6-3

MAHESH BHUPATHI (l) AND DANIELA HANTUCHOVA (r)

U.S. OPEN MIXED DOUBLES

PRIZE MONEY

Winner	$150,000	Quarterfinalists	15,000
Finalist	70,000	Round of 16	10,000
Semifinalists	30,000	Round of 32	5,000

First Round

BLACK, C./BLACK, W. (ZIM) (1)
FRAZIER, A./PARROTT, T. (USA) (WC)
SAFINA, D. (RUS)/RAM, A. (ISR)
HUSAROVA, J. (SVK)/FREIDL, L. (CZE)
STOSUR, S./HANLEY, P. (AUS)
KIRILENKO, M. (RUS)/OLIVER, G. (USA)
JANKOVIC, J. (SCG)/VIZNER, P. (CZE)
MOLIK, A./PERRY, T. (AUS) (8)
LIKHOVTSEVA, E. (RUS)/NESTOR, D. (CAN) (3)
SHAUGHNESSY, M./GIMELSTOB, J. (USA) (WC)
SREBOTNIK, K. (SLO)/ZIMONJIC (SCG)
STEWART, B. (AUS)/ERLICH, J. (ISR)
RUANO PASCUAL, V. (ESP)/HUSS, S. (AUS)
OSTERLOH, L./KIM, K. (USA) (WC)
GOLOVIN, T./SANTORO, F. (FRA)
NAVRATILOVA, M. (USA)/PAES, L. (IND) (7)
SUGIYAMA, A. (JPN)/ULLYETT, K. (ZIM) (5)
SALERNI, M.E./RODRIGUEZ, M. (ARG)
MEDINA GARRIGUES, A. (ESP)/ETLIS, G. (ARG)
GRANVILLE, L./LEACH, R. (USA) (WC)
SUN, T.T. (CHN)/ASPELIN, S. (SWE)
HANTUCHOVA, D. (SVK)/BHUPATHI, M. (IND)
PERRY, S./DELIC, A. (USA) (WC)
RAYMOND, L. (USA)/BJORKMAN, J. (SWE) (4)
MORARIU, C./BRYAN, M. (USA) (6)
CRAYBAS, J./MORRISON, J. (USA) (WC)
GROENEFELD, A.L. (GER)/CERMAK, F. (CZE)
PESCHKE, K./DAMM, M. (CZE)
PRATT, N. (AUS)/SUK, C. (CZE)
VAIDISOVA, N. (CZE)/KNOWLES, M. (BAH)
GARBIN, T. (ITA)/HOOD, M. (ARG)
STUBBS, R. (AUS)/BRYAN, B. (USA) (2)

Second Round

BLACK/BLACK 6-7(7), 6-3, 7-6(8)
SAFINA/RAM 6-1, 6-4
STOSUR/HANLEY 7-5, 6-4
MOLIK/PERRY 7-6(5), 2-6, 7-6(6)
LIKHOVTSEVA/NESTOR 6-4, 6-2
SREBOTNIK/ZIMONJIC 6-4, 6-2
RUANO PASCUAL/HUSS 7-6(1), 7-6(8)
NAVRATILOVA/PAES 6-3, 6-2
SUGIYAMA/ULLYETT 6-2, 6-3
MEDINA GARRIGUES/ETLIS 6-4, 6-2
HANTUCHOVA/BHUPATHI 4-6, 6-3, 7-6(9)
RAYMOND/BJORKMAN 6-1, 7-5
MORARIU/BRYAN 6-3, 6-4
GROENEFELD/CERMAK 6-7(5), 6-4, 7-6(7)
VAIDISOVA/KNOWLES 6-1, 1-6, 7-6(9)
STUBBS/BRYAN 6-2, 6-1

Quarterfinals

SAFINA/RAM 6-3, 6-4
STOSUR/HANLEY 7-6(1), 6-4
SREBOTNIK/ZIMONJIC 7-6(6), 6-3
NAVRATILOVA/PAES 6-4, 6-1
SUGIYAMA/ULLYETT 6-3, 6-4
HANTUCHOVA/BHUPATHI 6-2, 7-6(3)
MORARIU/BRYAN, M. 2-6, 6-2, 7-6(7)
STUBBS/BRYAN, B. 6-3, 7-6(4)

Semifinals

SAFINA/RAM 6-3, 6-4
SREBOTNIK/ZIMONJIC 7-6(2), 5-7, 7-6(9)
HANTUCHOVA/BHUPATHI 7-5, 6-2
MORARIU/BRYAN, M. 6-4, 6-4

Final

SREBOTNIK/ZIMONJIC 6-1, 7-5
HANTUCHOVA/BHUPATHI 7-6(4), 7-5

Champions

HANTUCHOVA/BHUPATHI 6-4, 6-2

VIKTORIA AZARENKA

JUNIOR DRAWS

NIKOLA FRANKOVA (l) AND ALISA KLEYBANOVA (r)

GIRLS' SINGLES

ROUND OF 16: Viktoria Azarenka (BLR) (1) d. Renee Reinhard (NED) 6-0, 6-0; **Marina Erakovic (NZL) (6)** d. **Vania King (USA) (10)** 6-3, 3-6, 7-6(2); **Mihaela Buzarnescu (ROM) (14)** d. Yaroslava Shvedova (RUS) 6-3, 6-3; Olga Govortsova (BLR) (Q) d. Sharon Fichman (CAN) 6-4, 6-4; **Alexa Glatch (USA) (7)** d. **Ekaterina Makarova (RUS) (9)** 7-6(2), 1-6, 6-3; **Dominika Cibulkova (SVK) (3)** d. **Bibiane Schoofs (NED) (13)** 6-3, 7-5; Nina Henkel (GER) d. **Wen-Hsin Hsu (TPE) (11)** 7-5, 1-6, 7-5; Elizabeth Plotkin (USA) d. Ekaterina Kosminskaya (RUS) (Q) 6-3, 6-4; **QUARTERFINALS: Azarenka** d. **Erakovic** 5-2 RET.; **Buzarnescu** d. Govortsova 6-2, 7-6(3); **Glatch** d. **Cibulkova** 6-0, 6-4; Henkel d. Plotkin 7-5, 7-5; **SEMIFINALS: Azarenka** d. **Buzarnescu** 3-6, 6-2, 6-2; **Glatch** d. Henkel 6-1, 7-5; **FINAL: Azarenka** d. **Glatch** 6-3, 6-4.

GIRLS' DOUBLES

DOUBLES QUARTERFINALS: Olga Govortsova (BLR)/Bibiane Schoofs (NED) d. **Viktoria Azarenka (BLR)/Marina Erakovic (NZL) (1)** W/O; **Nikola Frankova (CZE)/Alisa Kleybanova (RUS) (7)** d. **Mihaela Buzarnescu/ Alexandra Dulgheru (ROM) (3)** 6-3, 7-5; **Wen-Hsin Hsu (TPE)/Amina Rakhim (KAZ) (5)** d. **Anna Tatishvili (GEO)/Caroline Wozniacki (DEN) (4)** 5-7, 6-0, 7-5; **Alexa Glatch/Vania King (USA) (2)** d. Ayumi Morita/Erika Sema (JPN) 6-4, 6-3; **SEMIFINALS: Frankova/Kleybanova** d. Govortsova/Schoofs 7-6(6), 6-3; **Glatch/King** d. **Hsu/Rakhim** 6-3, 6-2; **FINAL: Frankova/Kleybanova** d. **Glatch/King** 7-5, 7-6(3).

RYAN SWEETING

DONALD YOUNG (l) AND ALEX CLAYTON (r)

BOYS' SINGLES

SINGLES ROUND OF 16: Donald Young (USA) (1) d. Matt Bruch (USA) (Q) 6-7(4), 7-6(4), 6-2; **Sun-Yong Kim (KOR) (6)** d. Christian Vitulli (KEN) 7-5, 6-4; **Leonardo Mayer (ARG) (3)** d. **Sam Querrey (USA) (13)** 7-6(4), 7-6(3); Ryan Sweeting (BAH) d. Holden Seguso (USA) (WC) 6-1, 6-2; Tim Smyczek (USA) d. **Alex Kuznetsov (USA) (5)** 7-6(3), 6-4; **Santiago Giraldo (COL) (4)** d. Piero Luisi (VEN) 6-2, 7-5; **Jeremy Chardy (FRA) (7)** d. Kei Nishikori (JPN) 7-5, 6-1; **Marin Cilic (CRO) (2) d. Evgeniy Kirillov (RUS) (14)** 7-6(5), 6-4; **QUARTERFINALS: Kim** d. **Young** 7-6(1), 2-6, 7-6(2); Sweeting d. **Mayer** 6-4, 7-5; **Giraldo** d. Smyczek 6-1, 3-6, 6-2; **Chardy** d. **Cilic** 4-6, 6-4, 6-2; **SEMIFINALS:** Sweeting d. **Kim** 6-4, 6-0; **Chardy** d. **Giraldo** 7-6(5); 6-2; **FINAL:** Sweeting d. **Chardy** 6-4, 6-4.

BOYS' DOUBLES

DOUBLES QUARTERFINALS: Alex Clayton/Donald Young (USA) (8) d. Kellen Damico/Tim Smyczek (USA) 6-1, 7-6(5); **Petar Jelenic (CRO)/Evgeniy Kirillov (RUS) (3)** d. **Timothy Neilly (USA)/Ryan Sweeting (BAH) (5)** 6-4, 1-6, 7-6(2); Jesse Levine/Michael Shabaz (USA) d. Pavol Cervenak/Lukas Lacko (SVK) 6-2, 7-6(2); **Carsten Ball (AUS)/Thiemo De Bakker (NED) (2)** d. Ivan Sergeyev (UKR)/Nikola Mektic (CRO) 2-6, 7-6(3), 7-6(5); **SEMIFINALS: Clayton/Young** d. **Jelenic/Kirillov** 6-2, 6-3; **Ball/De Bakker** d. Levine/Shabaz 6-1, 6-3; **FINAL: Clayton/Young** d. **Ball/De Bakker** 7-6(3), 4-6, 7-5.

SEE NO EVIL

by Lawrence Jeziak

A tennis fan following the 2005 U.S. Open on television might say the high point was Andre Agassi's come-from-behind, five-set tie-break victory over juggernaut James Blake. However, this viewer, along with a small but rapidly growing cult, would say the breathtaking picture quality of more than 100 hours of widescreen, high-definition broadcasts was even better.

HDTV is revolutionary. It also might be the most misunderstood application of 21st century communications. Aficionados call it awesome, comparing the leap from analog (the previous broadcasting standard) to digital high-definition as significant as the change from black-and-white to color telecasts. Cynics contend it is overrated and overpriced. One told me high definition is only a marketing ploy to increase sales of big-screen televisions.

ANDRE AGASSI (l) AND JAMES BLAKE (r)

As a member of the high-definition army since December 2004, I can testify to HD's spectacular picture quality. For tennis and other sporting events — considering the free parking, reasonably priced concessions and the absence of lines outside the restroom — it's better than a front row seat. For screening movies, it's better than going to the Cineplex.

However, like buying an automobile, a computer or a new tennis racquet, research is essential to finding an HDTV that fits your living situation, viewing habits and budget. Fortunately, there are a growing number of resources to reduce the confusion associated with purchasing an HDTV.

The web site www.inhd.com is a great place to start. INHD is a network available to high-definition cable subscribers with two channels featuring concerts, sporting events and movies — all in HD. For the last two years, it has presented the U.S. Clay Court Championships from Houston (produced by The Tennis Channel) and several World TeamTennis matches. But we'll focus on tennis and HDTV in a moment. First, an HDTV primer:

It is not necessary to refinance a mortgage to revolutionize your viewing area. While you can spend more than $10,000 for a home-theater system, I found a 46-inch Sony rear-projection HD monitor (requiring cable or satellite HD service), the matching Sony stand and a high-end Toshiba DVD player for less than $1,500. I did not purchase supplemental speakers; the television delivers impressive surround sound. In fact, Consumer Reports gives most rear-projection HDTVs its highest marks for sound.

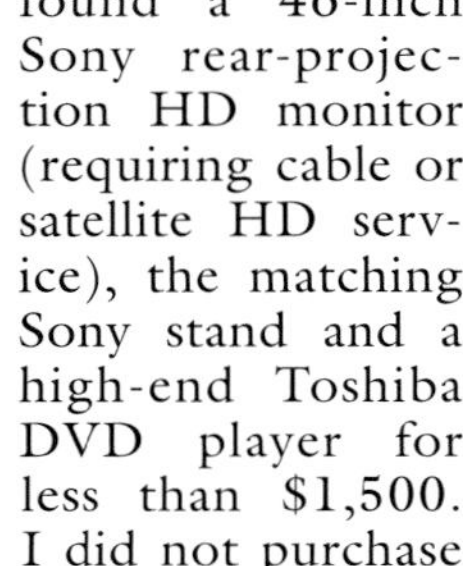

Rear-projection sets are rather bulky. My Sony weighs more than 100 pounds. A plasma screen, about as thick as a wide-body tennis racquet, can hang from the wall. A plasma screen also costs more than other HDTVs — a lot more. An LCD, while thicker than a plasma screen, delivers outstanding picture quality and is in the middle price range of high-definition options.

The INHD web site can also help one determine the appropriate size. And when talking about high-definition, size does matter. A common consumer error is buying a set that is too big. Like falling in love with a St. Bernard puppy, the 65-inch widescreen may be irresistible at the store. But if your viewing room forces you to sit too close to the screen, you won't enjoy it.

All digital sets deliver a great picture; the upgrade from analog is like looking out a window through freshly cleaned glass. But digital TV is not necessarily HDTV; changing from digital to high definition is like looking through the same window and removing the glass. According to Ken Aagaard, CBS's senior vice-president of operations and engineering, you will know when you are watching high definition: "You can't leave the set. It's the reason you don't hear about 3D anymore; this is it."

CBS is a leader in high-definition programming, presenting HD National Football League games since 1998, the U.S. Open in HD since 1999 and, this year, delivering 30 hours of HD prime-time programming each week. Aagaard calls HD tennis "sneaky good." Even before the USTA painted all the courts blue, you could easily see the ball in a high-definition telecast.

ESPN is also committed to high-definition programming. According to Bryan Burns, the network's vice-president of strategic business planning and development, ESPNHD is growing rapidly. Its 84 HD events in 2003 will expand to more than 500 in 2006, including the entire schedule of soccer's World Cup. And ESPN2HD, which launched this year, presented the Pilot Pen tennis tournament, the final event of the U.S. Open Series, in high-definition for the first time.

But even as HD programming increases, it remains an obstacle in the digital revolution. While 12 million households in the United States have at least one HDTV, fewer than half have HD service. According to Comcast, one of the nation's leading cable TV service providers, less than half of its 21 million subscribers have digital service, which, along with a $5 per month upgrade, is necessary for high-definition reception.

Even HD reception does not guarantee viewing HD programs. According to network spokespersons, ESPN2HD is "available" (if you have an HDTV and HD service) to only 20 percent of American households. Universal HD, the network that delivered USA Network's U.S. Open coverage in high definition — including complete, commercial-free re-airings of the Agassi-Blake match — is "available" to 30 million.

Cable and satellite providers alike are promising more HD channels. And according to ESPN's Burns, the Consumer Electronics Association is predicting that, for the first time, HDTVs sold in 2006 will outnumber lower-tech models. This is due to dropping prices as well as spreading the HDTV mantra: "Oh, wow!"

As far as tennis, there is little to suggest that HD coverage will come close to that given to football, baseball and basketball in the immediate future. Tennis will remain TV's stepchild. The Tennis Channel has no immediate plans to televise in high-definition. And when asked about bringing the other Grand Slam tournaments into the HD revolution, Burns replied, "It's hard to say." It's a question of logistics and planning, "like moving from checkers to three-dimensional chess."

And, according to Burns, the United States is ahead of Europe in delivering HD content. More than likely, similar to wanting live rather than tape-delayed matches, tennis fans will need to demand HD coverage.

Sure, you can still play tennis with a wooden racquet, listen to music on an 8-track deck, and watch movies on VHS tapes with a 13-inch black-and-white television, but as Bill Macatee observed during CBS's Labor Day coverage of the Open, "If you are watching this in high definition, you are loving life."

High-definition is the future. And for some, the future is now.

THE COMEBACK KID

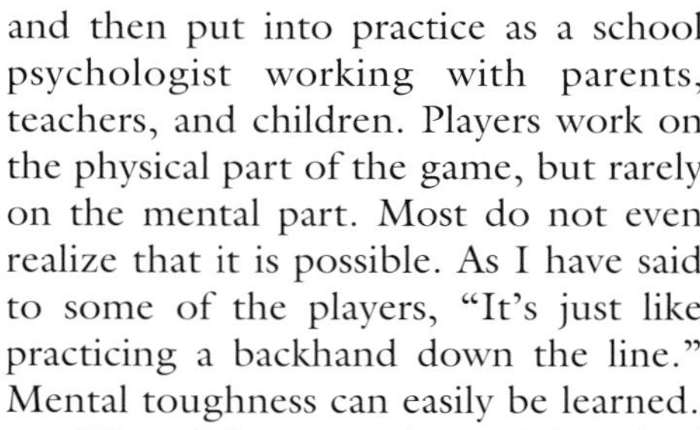

by Anne Smith, Ph.D.

At age 46, with 10 Grand Slam championships on my resume, I am making a comeback to professional tennis. Why? Why now? My passion and love for the game are still there; and I do not want to look back ever and ask myself why I didn't try.

Believe me, I do not like to lose. But the greatest loss of all is not trying. People have asked me, "Why don't you just play doubles?" That's what I am noted for, since I have won more than 30 WTA Tour doubles titles. Playing singles is a challenge and also helps my doubles game. Besides, my highest singles ranking was No. 12 in the world. This time, however, I am doing it differently. I have given up the idea that I have to be perfect. I now spend my time enjoying the game. Focusing on mistakes and what I'm not doing well reinforces and creates more mistakes. It becomes a vicious cycle. Focusing on what I am doing well helps create a winning mindset and enhances my performance. It is also much more fun.

ANNE SMITH

The game has changed significantly since I last played competitively in 1991. There is more of an emphasis on power, although Monica Seles, for example, could hit the ball as hard as any of the current players. But the game is so much more than hitting the ball. It's also about the mental aspects. This is where I use what I learned studying for my Ph.D. in educational psychology and then put into practice as a school psychologist working with parents, teachers, and children. Players work on the physical part of the game, but rarely on the mental part. Most do not even realize that it is possible. As I have said to some of the players, "It's just like practicing a backhand down the line." Mental toughness can easily be learned.

When I first started out, I thought I could go in and win matches. I found out that that was not going to happen. I had been out of the game for 14 years, and there is no substitute for match play. Most of these young players had been playing on the USTA/ITF tour for several years and were match tough. So I went from focusing on winning matches to winning points. This change brought back thoughts and feelings from when I was on the tour. It made me realize that everything I had back then to make me a champion was still inside of me; I just needed to give it time to come out. There are no short cuts. So, eventually, I started winning points, then games, then sets, then matches and then a tournament.

There were times in the beginning, when I was losing badly in singles, that I was having second thoughts about my comeback. I decided to just keep working on my game, trying to improve every time I stepped on the court, and focusing on the love of the game rather than on winning and losing. I started having more fun and my game improved. Something else that kept me going was the player and fan reaction to me. The fans at all the circuit stops have been great. They don't care if I win or lose; they just want to see me play. They say it gives them hope. The tour players have encouraged me to stay by saying, "You only need more match experience." This made a huge difference for me. In nine tournaments, I have reached the semifinals in doubles four times and won my first doubles title in July in Southlake, Texas, with Tara Snyder.

When I first started on the USTA Pro Circuit in February, I had just resigned from a full-time position as the director of the Learning Center at Dean College in Franklin, Mass. I had not been able to train and practice as much as I had wanted and had no idea what to expect from my game or the other players. At first, I tried to play the "modern game," hitting the ball hard and staying on the baseline. Then I realized that it was best for me if I played my own game. I have a slice backhand and I can hit off-pace with my forehand, and I discovered that the players didn't like these shots. They like to hit hard balls that come waist high. So my "retro" game worked well. My game, combined with the tweaking of my court movement and more simplified training, has really helped my play come together. And women 20 years my junior were not only welcoming, they even wanted to hit and play doubles with me.

Having a supportive and empowering coach has also made a significant difference in my game and desire to play again at the professional level. Bev Raws has a style of coaching that has helped make the game fun for me. Together, we have developed a program based on the things that have helped me in my comeback and that we use at the Boston Athletic Club when we work with junior players, adult club players and tour players. This program is based on empowering coaching and creates a winning mindset and environment. It involves a combination of technique, martial arts, psychology, metaphysics and "cueing." The same concepts that have helped me can be applied to any level of player. We have had great results and the concepts are simple and easy to teach.

I have committed to playing at least two more years on the women's professional circuit. I will continue to play both singles and doubles, with my goal being to play on the WTA Tour again. My comeback has done so much for me on both an inner and personal gratification level. As I recently said in an interview, winning 10 Grand Slam tournament titles is incredible; getting a second chance to play the game I love......priceless!

MARAT SAFIN

2005 AUSTRALIAN OPEN

MEN'S SINGLES

JANUARY 17-30 • MELBOURNE, AUSTRALIA • REBOUND ACE

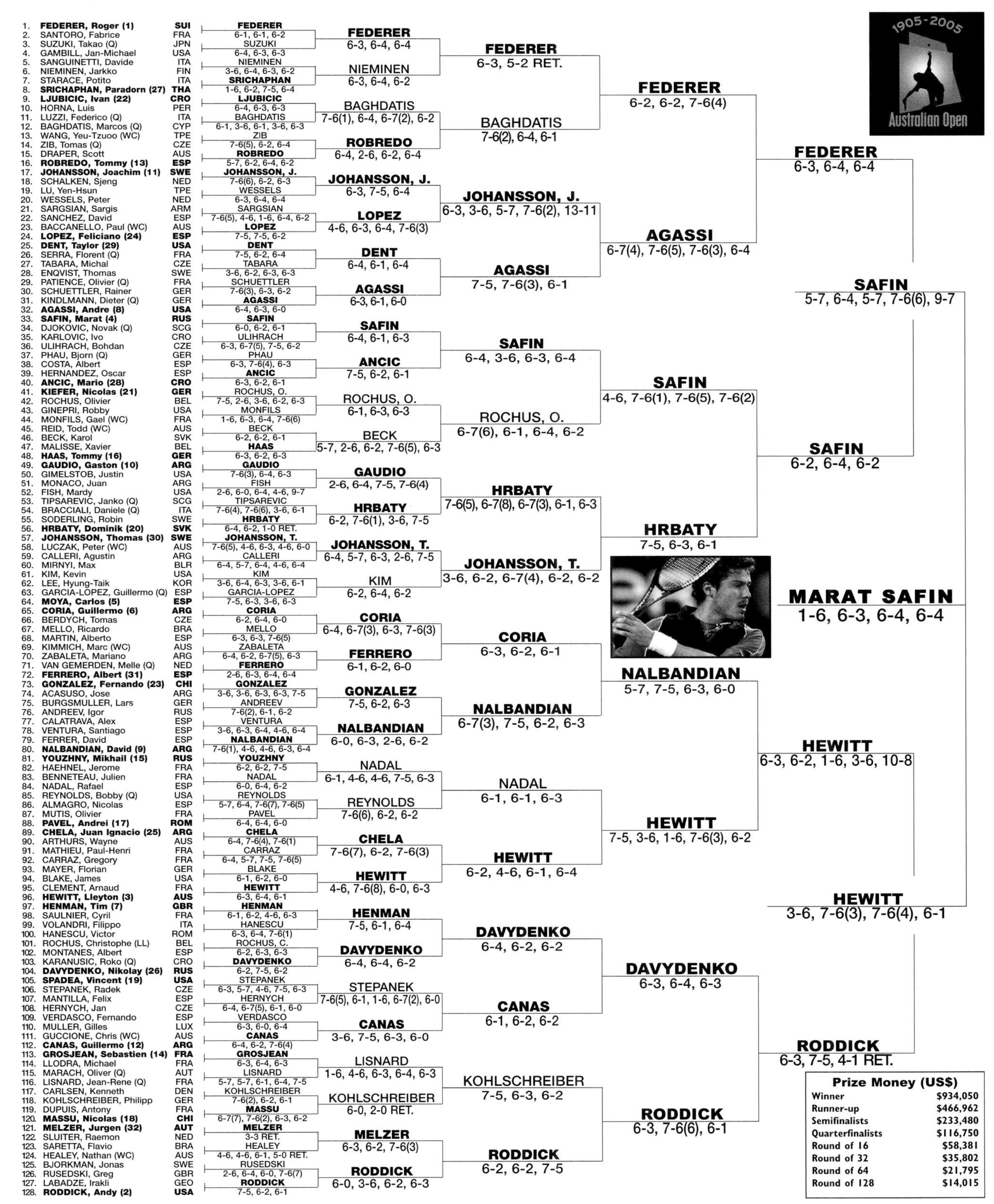

Draw

1.	**FEDERER, Roger (1)**	**SUI**
2.	SANTORO, Fabrice	FRA
3.	SUZUKI, Takao (Q)	JPN
4.	GAMBILL, Jan-Michael	USA
5.	SANGUINETTI, Davide	ITA
6.	NIEMINEN, Jarkko	FIN
7.	STARACE, Potito	ITA
8.	**SRICHAPHAN, Paradorn (27)**	**THA**
9.	**LJUBICIC, Ivan (22)**	**CRO**
10.	HORNA, Luis	PER
11.	LUZZI, Federico (Q)	ITA
12.	BAGHDATIS, Marcos (Q)	CYP
13.	WANG, Yeu-Tzuoo (WC)	TPE
14.	ZIB, Tomas (Q)	CZE
15.	DRAPER, Scott	AUS
16.	**ROBREDO, Tommy (13)**	**ESP**
17.	**JOHANSSON, Joachim (11)**	**SWE**
18.	SCHALKEN, Sjeng	NED
19.	LU, Yen-Hsun	TPE
20.	WESSELS, Peter	NED
21.	SARGSIAN, Sargis	ARM
22.	SANCHEZ, David	ESP
23.	BACCANELLO, Paul (WC)	AUS
24.	**LOPEZ, Feliciano (24)**	**ESP**
25.	**DENT, Taylor (29)**	**USA**
26.	SERRA, Florent (Q)	FRA
27.	TABARA, Michal	CZE
28.	ENQVIST, Thomas	SWE
29.	PATIENCE, Olivier (Q)	FRA
30.	SCHUETTLER, Rainer	GER
31.	KINDLMANN, Dieter (Q)	GER
32.	**AGASSI, Andre (8)**	**USA**
33.	**SAFIN, Marat (4)**	**RUS**
34.	DJOKOVIC, Novak (Q)	SCG
35.	KARLOVIC, Ivo	CRO
36.	ULIHRACH, Bohdan	CZE
37.	PHAU, Bjorn (Q)	GER
38.	COSTA, Albert	ESP
39.	HERNANDEZ, Oscar	ESP
40.	**ANCIC, Mario (28)**	**CRO**
41.	**KIEFER, Nicolas (21)**	**GER**
42.	ROCHUS, Olivier	BEL
43.	GINEPRI, Robby	USA
44.	MONFILS, Gael (WC)	FRA
45.	REID, Todd (WC)	AUS
46.	BECK, Karol	SVK
47.	MALISSE, Xavier	BEL
48.	**HAAS, Tommy (16)**	**GER**
49.	**GAUDIO, Gaston (10)**	**ARG**
50.	GIMELSTOB, Justin	USA
51.	MONACO, Juan	ARG
52.	FISH, Mardy	USA
53.	TIPSAREVIC, Janko (Q)	SCG
54.	BRACCIALI, Daniele (Q)	ITA
55.	SODERLING, Robin	SWE
56.	**HRBATY, Dominik (20)**	**SVK**
57.	**JOHANSSON, Thomas (30)**	**SWE**
58.	LUCZAK, Peter (WC)	AUS
59.	CALLERI, Agustin	ARG
60.	MIRNYI, Max	BLR
61.	KIM, Kevin	USA
62.	LEE, Hyung-Taik	KOR
63.	GARCIA-LOPEZ, Guillermo (Q)	ESP
64.	**MOYA, Carlos (5)**	**ESP**
65.	**CORIA, Guillermo (6)**	**ARG**
66.	BERDYCH, Tomas	CZE
67.	MELLO, Ricardo	BRA
68.	MARTIN, Alberto	ESP
69.	KIMMICH, Marc (WC)	AUS
70.	ZABALETA, Mariano	ARG
71.	VAN GEMERDEN, Melle (Q)	NED
72.	**FERRERO, Albert (31)**	**ESP**
73.	**GONZALEZ, Fernando (23)**	**CHI**
74.	ACASUSO, Jose	ARG
75.	BURGSMULLER, Lars	GER
76.	ANDREEV, Igor	RUS
77.	CALATRAVA, Alex	ESP
78.	VENTURA, Santiago	ESP
79.	FERRER, David	ESP
80.	**NALBANDIAN, David (9)**	**ARG**
81.	**YOUZHNY, Mikhail (15)**	**RUS**
82.	HAEHNEL, Jerome	FRA
83.	BENNETEAU, Julien	FRA
84.	NADAL, Rafael	ESP
85.	REYNOLDS, Bobby (Q)	USA
86.	ALMAGRO, Nicolas	ESP
87.	MUTIS, Olivier	FRA
88.	**PAVEL, Andrei (17)**	**ROM**
89.	**CHELA, Juan Ignacio (25)**	**ARG**
90.	ARTHURS, Wayne	AUS
91.	MATHIEU, Paul-Henri	FRA
92.	CARRAZ, Gregory	FRA
93.	MAYER, Florian	GER
94.	BLAKE, James	USA
95.	CLEMENT, Arnaud	FRA
96.	**HEWITT, Lleyton (3)**	**AUS**
97.	**HENMAN, Tim (7)**	**GBR**
98.	SAULNIER, Cyril	FRA
99.	VOLANDRI, Filippo	ITA
100.	HANESCU, Victor	ROM
101.	ROCHUS, Christophe (LL)	BEL
102.	MONTANES, Albert	ESP
103.	KARANUSIC, Roko (Q)	CRO
104.	**DAVYDENKO, Nikolay (26)**	**RUS**
105.	**SPADEA, Vincent (19)**	**USA**
106.	STEPANEK, Radek	CZE
107.	MANTILLA, Felix	ESP
108.	HERNYCH, Jan	CZE
109.	VERDASCO, Fernando	ESP
110.	MULLER, Gilles	LUX
111.	GUCCIONE, Chris (WC)	AUS
112.	**CANAS, Guillermo (12)**	**ARG**
113.	**GROSJEAN, Sebastien (14)**	**FRA**
114.	LLODRA, Michael	FRA
115.	MARACH, Oliver (Q)	AUT
116.	LISNARD, Jean-Rene (Q)	FRA
117.	CARLSEN, Kenneth	DEN
118.	KOHLSCHREIBER, Philipp	GER
119.	DUPUIS, Antony	FRA
120.	**MASSU, Nicolas (18)**	**CHI**
121.	**MELZER, Jurgen (32)**	**AUT**
122.	SLUITER, Raemon	NED
123.	SARETTA, Flavio	BRA
124.	HEALEY, Nathan (WC)	AUS
125.	BJORKMAN, Jonas	SWE
126.	RUSEDSKI, Greg	GBR
127.	LABADZE, Irakli	GEO
128.	**RODDICK, Andy (2)**	**USA**

First Round

FEDERER 6-1, 6-1, 6-2
SUZUKI 6-4, 6-3, 6-3
NIEMINEN 3-6, 6-4, 6-3, 6-2
SRICHAPHAN 1-6, 6-2, 7-5, 6-4
LJUBICIC 6-4, 6-3, 6-3
BAGHDATIS 6-1, 3-6, 6-1, 3-6, 6-3
ZIB 7-6(5), 6-2, 6-4
ROBREDO 5-7, 6-2, 6-4, 6-2
JOHANSSON, J. 7-6(6), 6-2, 6-3
WESSELS 6-3, 6-4, 6-4
SARGSIAN 7-6(5), 4-6, 1-6, 6-4, 6-2
LOPEZ 7-5, 7-5, 6-2
DENT 7-5, 6-2, 6-4
TABARA 3-6, 6-2, 6-3, 6-3
SCHUETTLER 7-6(3), 6-3, 6-2
AGASSI 6-4, 6-3, 6-0
SAFIN 6-0, 6-2, 6-1
ULIHRACH 6-3, 6-7(5), 7-5, 6-2
PHAU 6-3, 7-6(4), 6-3
ANCIC 6-3, 6-2, 6-1
ROCHUS, O. 7-5, 2-6, 3-6, 6-2, 6-3
MONFILS 1-6, 6-3, 6-4, 7-6(6)
BECK 6-2, 6-2, 6-1
HAAS 6-3, 6-2, 6-3
GAUDIO 7-6(3), 6-4, 6-3
FISH 2-6, 6-0, 6-4, 4-6, 9-7
TIPSAREVIC 7-6(4), 7-6(6), 3-6, 6-1
HRBATY 6-4, 6-2, 1-0 RET.
JOHANSSON, T. 7-6(5), 4-6, 6-3, 4-6, 6-0
CALLERI 6-4, 5-7, 6-4, 4-6, 6-4
KIM 3-6, 6-4, 6-3, 3-6, 6-1
GARCIA-LOPEZ 7-5, 6-3, 3-6, 6-3
CORIA 6-2, 6-4, 6-0
MELLO 6-3, 6-3, 7-6(5)
ZABALETA 6-4, 6-2, 6-7(5), 6-3
FERRERO 2-6, 6-3, 6-4, 6-4
GONZALEZ 3-6, 3-6, 6-3, 6-3, 7-5
ANDREEV 7-6(2), 6-1, 6-2
VENTURA 3-6, 6-3, 6-4, 4-6, 6-4
NALBANDIAN 7-6(1), 4-6, 4-6, 6-3, 6-4
YOUZHNY 6-2, 6-2, 7-5
NADAL 6-0, 6-4, 6-2
REYNOLDS 5-7, 6-4, 7-6(7), 7-6(5)
PAVEL 6-4, 6-4, 6-0
CHELA 6-4, 7-6(4), 7-6(1)
CARRAZ 6-4, 5-7, 7-5, 7-6(5)
BLAKE 6-1, 6-2, 6-0
HEWITT 6-3, 6-4, 6-1
HENMAN 6-1, 6-2, 4-6, 6-3
HANESCU 6-3, 6-4, 7-6(1)
ROCHUS, C. 6-2, 6-3, 6-3
DAVYDENKO 6-2, 7-5, 6-2
STEPANEK 6-3, 5-7, 4-6, 7-5, 6-3
HERNYCH 6-4, 6-7(5), 6-1, 6-0
VERDASCO 6-3, 6-0, 6-4
CANAS 6-4, 6-2, 7-6(4)
GROSJEAN 6-3, 6-4, 6-3
LISNARD 5-7, 5-7, 6-1, 6-4, 7-5
KOHLSCHREIBER 7-6(2), 6-2, 6-1
MASSU 6-7(7), 7-6(2), 6-3, 6-2
MELZER 3-3 RET.
HEALEY 4-6, 4-6, 6-1, 5-0 RET.
RUSEDSKI 2-6, 6-4, 6-0, 7-6(7)
RODDICK 7-5, 6-2, 6-1

Second Round

FEDERER 6-3, 6-4, 6-4
NIEMINEN 6-3, 6-4, 6-2
BAGHDATIS 7-6(1), 6-4, 6-7(2), 6-2
ROBREDO 6-4, 2-6, 6-2, 6-4
JOHANSSON, J. 6-3, 7-5, 6-4
LOPEZ 4-6, 6-3, 6-4, 7-6(3)
DENT 6-4, 6-1, 6-4
AGASSI 6-3, 6-1, 6-0
SAFIN 6-4, 6-1, 6-3
ANCIC 7-5, 6-2, 6-1
ROCHUS, O. 6-1, 6-3, 6-3
BECK 5-7, 2-6, 6-2, 7-6(5), 6-3
GAUDIO 2-6, 6-4, 7-5, 7-6(4)
HRBATY 6-2, 7-6(1), 3-6, 7-5
JOHANSSON, T. 6-4, 5-7, 6-3, 2-6, 7-5
KIM 6-2, 6-4, 6-2
CORIA 6-4, 6-7(3), 6-3, 7-6(3)
FERRERO 6-1, 6-2, 6-0
GONZALEZ 7-5, 6-2, 6-3
NALBANDIAN 6-0, 6-3, 2-6, 6-2
NADAL 6-1, 4-6, 4-6, 7-5, 6-3
REYNOLDS 7-6(6), 6-2, 6-2
CHELA 7-6(7), 6-2, 7-6(3)
HEWITT 4-6, 7-6(8), 6-0, 6-3
HENMAN 7-5, 6-1, 6-4
DAVYDENKO 6-4, 6-4, 6-2
STEPANEK 7-6(5), 6-1, 1-6, 6-7(2), 6-0
CANAS 3-6, 7-5, 6-3, 6-0
LISNARD 1-6, 4-6, 6-3, 6-4, 6-3
KOHLSCHREIBER 6-0, 2-0 RET.
MELZER 6-3, 6-2, 7-6(3)
RODDICK 6-0, 3-6, 6-2, 6-3

Third Round

FEDERER 6-3, 5-2 RET.
BAGHDATIS 7-6(2), 6-4, 6-1
JOHANSSON, J. 6-3, 3-6, 5-7, 7-6(2), 13-11
AGASSI 7-5, 7-6(3), 6-1
SAFIN 6-4, 3-6, 6-3, 6-4
ROCHUS, O. 6-7(6), 6-1, 6-4, 6-2
HRBATY 7-6(5), 6-7(8), 6-7(3), 6-1, 6-3
JOHANSSON, T. 3-6, 6-2, 6-7(4), 6-2, 6-2
CORIA 6-3, 6-2, 6-1
NALBANDIAN 6-7(3), 7-5, 6-2, 6-3
NADAL 6-1, 6-1, 6-3
HEWITT 6-2, 4-6, 6-1, 6-4
DAVYDENKO 6-4, 6-2, 6-2
CANAS 6-1, 6-2, 6-2
KOHLSCHREIBER 7-5, 6-3, 6-2
RODDICK 6-2, 6-2, 7-5

Fourth Round

FEDERER 6-2, 6-2, 7-6(4)
AGASSI 6-7(4), 7-6(5), 7-6(3), 6-4
SAFIN 4-6, 7-6(1), 7-6(5), 7-6(2)
HRBATY 7-5, 6-3, 6-1
NALBANDIAN 5-7, 7-5, 6-3, 6-0
HEWITT 7-5, 3-6, 1-6, 7-6(3), 6-2
DAVYDENKO 6-3, 6-4, 6-3
RODDICK 6-3, 7-6(6), 6-1

Quarterfinals

FEDERER 6-3, 6-4, 6-4
SAFIN 6-2, 6-4, 6-2
HEWITT 6-3, 6-2, 1-6, 3-6, 10-8
RODDICK 6-3, 7-5, 4-1 RET.

Semifinals

SAFIN 5-7, 6-4, 5-7, 7-6(6), 9-7
HEWITT 3-6, 7-6(3), 7-6(4), 6-1

Final

MARAT SAFIN 1-6, 6-3, 6-4, 6-4

Prize Money (US$)

Winner	$934,050
Runner-up	$466,962
Semifinalists	$233,480
Quarterfinalists	$116,750
Round of 16	$58,381
Round of 32	$35,802
Round of 64	$21,795
Round of 128	$14,015

SERENA WILLIAMS

2005 AUSTRALIAN OPEN

WOMEN'S SINGLES

JANUARY 17 -30 • MELBOURNE, AUSTRALIA • REBOUND ACE

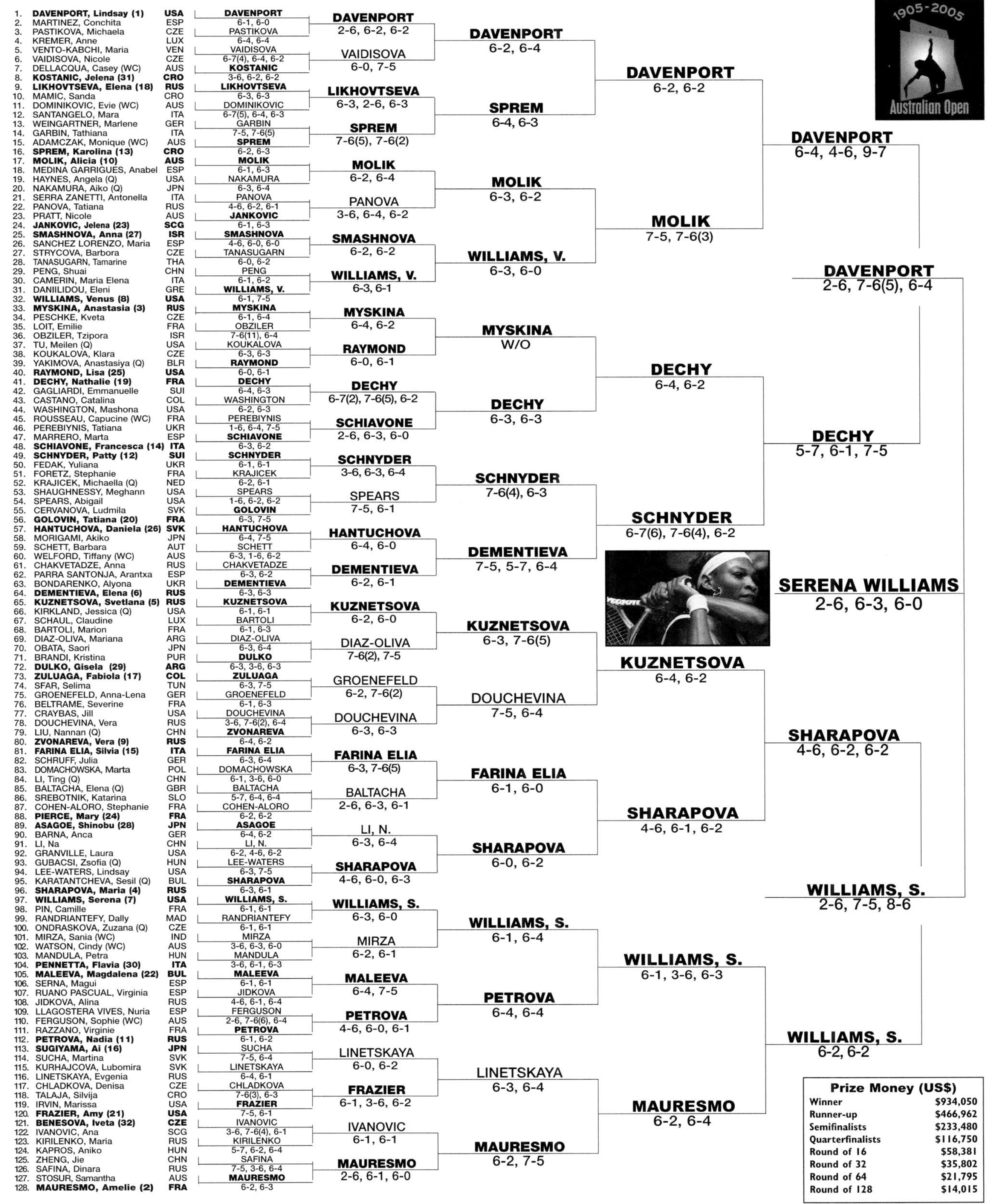

1.	**DAVENPORT, Lindsay (1)**	**USA**
2.	MARTINEZ, Conchita	ESP
3.	PASTIKOVA, Michaela	CZE
4.	KREMER, Anne	LUX
5.	VENTO-KABCHI, Maria	VEN
6.	VAIDISOVA, Nicole	CZE
7.	DELLACQUA, Casey (WC)	AUS
8.	**KOSTANIC, Jelena (31)**	**CRO**
9.	**LIKHOVTSEVA, Elena (18)**	**RUS**
10.	MAMIC, Sanda	CRO
11.	DOMINIKOVIC, Evie (WC)	AUS
12.	SANTANGELO, Mara	ITA
13.	WEINGARTNER, Marlene	GER
14.	GARBIN, Tathiana	ITA
15.	ADAMCZAK, Monique (WC)	AUS
16.	**SPREM, Karolina (13)**	**CRO**
17.	**MOLIK, Alicia (10)**	**AUS**
18.	MEDINA GARRIGUES, Anabel	ESP
19.	HAYNES, Angela (Q)	USA
20.	NAKAMURA, Aiko (Q)	JPN
21.	SERRA ZANETTI, Antonella	ITA
22.	PANOVA, Tatiana	RUS
23.	PRATT, Nicole	AUS
24.	**JANKOVIC, Jelena (23)**	**SCG**
25.	**SMASHNOVA, Anna (27)**	**ISR**
26.	SANCHEZ LORENZO, Maria	ESP
27.	STRYCOVA, Barbora	CZE
28.	TANASUGARN, Tamarine	THA
29.	PENG, Shuai	CHN
30.	CAMERIN, Maria Elena	ITA
31.	DANIILIDOU, Eleni	GRE
32.	**WILLIAMS, Venus (8)**	**USA**
33.	**MYSKINA, Anastasia (3)**	**RUS**
34.	PESCHKE, Kveta	CZE
35.	LOIT, Emilie	FRA
36.	OBZILER, Tzipora	ISR
37.	TU, Meilen (Q)	USA
38.	KOUKALOVA, Klara	CZE
39.	YAKIMOVA, Anastasiya (Q)	BLR
40.	**RAYMOND, Lisa (25)**	**USA**
41.	**DECHY, Nathalie (19)**	**FRA**
42.	GAGLIARDI, Emmanuelle	SUI
43.	CASTANO, Catalina	COL
44.	WASHINGTON, Mashona	USA
45.	ROUSSEAU, Capucine (WC)	FRA
46.	PEREBIYNIS, Tatiana	UKR
47.	MARRERO, Marta	ESP
48.	**SCHIAVONE, Francesca (14)**	**ITA**
49.	**SCHNYDER, Patty (12)**	**SUI**
50.	FEDAK, Yuliana	UKR
51.	FORETZ, Stephanie	FRA
52.	KRAJICEK, Michaella (Q)	NED
53.	SHAUGHNESSY, Meghann	USA
54.	SPEARS, Abigail	USA
55.	CERVANOVA, Ludmila	SVK
56.	**GOLOVIN, Tatiana (20)**	**FRA**
57.	**HANTUCHOVA, Daniela (26)**	**SVK**
58.	MORIGAMI, Akiko	JPN
59.	SCHETT, Barbara	AUT
60.	WELFORD, Tiffany (WC)	AUS
61.	CHAKVETADZE, Anna	RUS
62.	PARRA SANTONJA, Arantxa	ESP
63.	BONDARENKO, Alyona	UKR
64.	**DEMENTIEVA, Elena (6)**	**RUS**
65.	**KUZNETSOVA, Svetlana (5)**	**RUS**
66.	KIRKLAND, Jessica (Q)	USA
67.	SCHAUL, Claudine	LUX
68.	BARTOLI, Marion	FRA
69.	DIAZ-OLIVA, Mariana	ARG
70.	OBATA, Saori	JPN
71.	BRANDI, Kristina	PUR
72.	**DULKO, Gisela (29)**	**ARG**
73.	**ZULUAGA, Fabiola (17)**	**COL**
74.	SFAR, Selima	TUN
75.	GROENEFELD, Anna-Lena	GER
76.	BELTRAME, Severine	FRA
77.	CRAYBAS, Jill	USA
78.	DOUCHEVINA, Vera	RUS
79.	LIU, Nannan (Q)	CHN
80.	**ZVONAREVA, Vera (9)**	**RUS**
81.	**FARINA ELIA, Silvia (15)**	**ITA**
82.	SCHRUFF, Julia	GER
83.	DOMACHOWSKA, Marta	POL
84.	LI, Ting (Q)	CHN
85.	BALTACHA, Elena (Q)	GBR
86.	SREBOTNIK, Katarina	SLO
87.	COHEN-ALORO, Stephanie	FRA
88.	**PIERCE, Mary (24)**	**FRA**
89.	**ASAGOE, Shinobu (28)**	**JPN**
90.	BARNA, Anca	GER
91.	LI, Na	CHN
92.	GRANVILLE, Laura	USA
93.	GUBACSI, Zsofia (Q)	HUN
94.	LEE-WATERS, Lindsay	USA
95.	KARATANTCHEVA, Sesil (Q)	BUL
96.	**SHARAPOVA, Maria (4)**	**RUS**
97.	**WILLIAMS, Serena (7)**	**USA**
98.	PIN, Camille	FRA
99.	RANDRIANTEFY, Dally	MAD
100.	ONDRASKOVA, Zuzana (Q)	CZE
101.	MIRZA, Sania (WC)	IND
102.	WATSON, Cindy (WC)	AUS
103.	MANDULA, Petra	HUN
104.	**PENNETTA, Flavia (30)**	**ITA**
105.	**MALEEVA, Magdalena (22)**	**BUL**
106.	SERNA, Magui	ESP
107.	RUANO PASCUAL, Virginia	ESP
108.	JIDKOVA, Alina	RUS
109.	LLAGOSTERA VIVES, Nuria	ESP
110.	FERGUSON, Sophie (WC)	AUS
111.	RAZZANO, Virginie	FRA
112.	**PETROVA, Nadia (11)**	**RUS**
113.	**SUGIYAMA, Ai (16)**	**JPN**
114.	SUCHA, Martina	SVK
115.	KURHAJCOVA, Lubomira	SVK
116.	LINETSKAYA, Evgenia	RUS
117.	CHLADKOVA, Denisa	CZE
118.	TALAJA, Silvija	CRO
119.	IRVIN, Marissa	USA
120.	**FRAZIER, Amy (21)**	**USA**
121.	**BENESOVA, Iveta (32)**	**CZE**
122.	IVANOVIC, Ana	SCG
123.	KIRILENKO, Maria	RUS
124.	KAPROS, Aniko	HUN
125.	ZHENG, Jie	CHN
126.	SAFINA, Dinara	RUS
127.	STOSUR, Samantha	AUS
128.	**MAURESMO, Amelie (2)**	**FRA**

First round

- **DAVENPORT** 6-1, 6-0
- PASTIKOVA 6-4, 6-4
- VAIDISOVA 6-7(4), 6-4, 6-2
- **KOSTANIC** 3-6, 6-2, 6-2
- **LIKHOVTSEVA** 6-3, 6-3
- DOMINIKOVIC 6-7(5), 6-4, 6-3
- GARBIN 7-5, 7-6(5)
- **SPREM** 6-2, 6-3
- **MOLIK** 6-1, 6-3
- NAKAMURA 6-3, 6-4
- PANOVA 4-6, 6-2, 6-1
- **JANKOVIC** 6-1, 6-3
- **SMASHNOVA** 4-6, 6-0, 6-0
- TANASUGARN 6-0, 6-2
- PENG 6-1, 6-2
- **WILLIAMS, V.** 6-1, 7-5
- **MYSKINA** 6-1, 6-4
- OBZILER 7-6(11), 6-4
- KOUKALOVA 6-3, 6-3
- **RAYMOND** 6-0, 6-1
- **DECHY** 6-4, 6-3
- WASHINGTON 6-2, 6-3
- PEREBIYNIS 1-6, 6-4, 7-5
- **SCHIAVONE** 6-3, 6-2
- **SCHNYDER** 6-1, 6-1
- KRAJICEK 6-2, 6-1
- SPEARS 1-6, 6-2, 6-2
- **GOLOVIN** 6-3, 7-5
- **HANTUCHOVA** 6-4, 7-5
- SCHETT 6-3, 1-6, 6-2
- CHAKVETADZE 6-3, 6-2
- **DEMENTIEVA** 6-3, 6-3
- **KUZNETSOVA** 6-1, 6-1
- BARTOLI 6-1, 6-3
- DIAZ-OLIVA 6-3, 6-4
- **DULKO** 6-3, 3-6, 6-3
- **ZULUAGA** 6-3, 7-5
- GROENEFELD 6-1, 6-3
- DOUCHEVINA 3-6, 7-6(2), 6-4
- **ZVONAREVA** 6-4, 6-2
- **FARINA ELIA** 6-3, 6-4
- DOMACHOWSKA 6-1, 3-6, 6-0
- BALTACHA 5-7, 6-4, 6-4
- COHEN-ALORO 6-2, 6-2
- **ASAGOE** 6-4, 6-2
- LI, N. 6-2, 4-6, 6-2
- LEE-WATERS 6-3, 7-5
- **SHARAPOVA** 6-3, 6-1
- **WILLIAMS, S.** 6-1, 6-1
- RANDRIANTEFY 6-1, 6-1
- MIRZA 3-6, 6-3, 6-0
- MANDULA 3-6, 6-1, 6-3
- **MALEEVA** 6-1, 6-1
- JIDKOVA 4-6, 6-1, 6-4
- FERGUSON 2-6, 7-6(6), 6-4
- **PETROVA** 6-1, 6-2
- SUCHA 7-5, 6-4
- LINETSKAYA 6-4, 6-1
- CHLADKOVA 7-6(3), 6-3
- **FRAZIER** 7-5, 6-1
- IVANOVIC 3-6, 7-6(4), 6-1
- KIRILENKO 5-7, 6-2, 6-4
- SAFINA 7-5, 3-6, 6-4
- **MAURESMO** 6-2, 6-3

Second round

- **DAVENPORT** 2-6, 6-2, 6-2
- VAIDISOVA 6-0, 7-5
- **LIKHOVTSEVA** 6-3, 2-6, 6-3
- **SPREM** 7-6(5), 7-6(2)
- **MOLIK** 6-2, 6-4
- PANOVA 3-6, 6-4, 6-2
- **SMASHNOVA** 6-2, 6-2
- **WILLIAMS, V.** 6-3, 6-1
- **MYSKINA** 6-4, 6-2
- **RAYMOND** 6-0, 6-1
- **DECHY** 6-7(2), 7-6(5), 6-2
- **SCHIAVONE** 2-6, 6-3, 6-0
- **SCHNYDER** 3-6, 6-3, 6-4
- SPEARS 7-5, 6-1
- **HANTUCHOVA** 6-4, 6-0
- **DEMENTIEVA** 6-2, 6-1
- **KUZNETSOVA** 6-2, 6-0
- DIAZ-OLIVA 7-6(2), 7-5
- GROENEFELD 6-2, 7-6(2)
- DOUCHEVINA 6-3, 6-3
- **FARINA ELIA** 6-3, 7-6(5)
- BALTACHA 2-6, 6-3, 6-1
- LI, N. 6-3, 6-4
- **SHARAPOVA** 4-6, 6-0, 6-3
- **WILLIAMS, S.** 6-3, 6-0
- MIRZA 6-2, 6-1
- **MALEEVA** 6-4, 7-5
- **PETROVA** 4-6, 6-0, 6-1
- LINETSKAYA 6-0, 6-2
- **FRAZIER** 6-1, 3-6, 6-2
- IVANOVIC 6-1, 6-1
- **MAURESMO** 2-6, 6-1, 6-0

Third round

- **DAVENPORT** 6-2, 6-4
- **SPREM** 6-4, 6-3
- **MOLIK** 6-3, 6-2
- **WILLIAMS, V.** 6-3, 6-0
- **MYSKINA** W/O
- **DECHY** 6-3, 6-3
- **SCHNYDER** 7-6(4), 6-3
- **DEMENTIEVA** 7-5, 5-7, 6-4
- **KUZNETSOVA** 6-3, 7-6(5)
- DOUCHEVINA 7-5, 6-4
- **FARINA ELIA** 6-1, 6-0
- **SHARAPOVA** 6-0, 6-2
- **WILLIAMS, S.** 6-1, 6-4
- **PETROVA** 6-4, 6-4
- LINETSKAYA 6-3, 6-4
- **MAURESMO** 6-2, 7-5

Fourth round

- **DAVENPORT** 6-2, 6-2
- **MOLIK** 7-5, 7-6(3)
- **DECHY** 6-4, 6-2
- **SCHNYDER** 6-7(6), 7-6(4), 6-2
- **KUZNETSOVA** 6-4, 6-2
- **SHARAPOVA** 4-6, 6-1, 6-2
- **WILLIAMS, S.** 6-1, 3-6, 6-3
- **MAURESMO** 6-2, 6-4

Quarterfinals

- **DAVENPORT** 6-4, 4-6, 9-7
- **DECHY** 5-7, 6-1, 7-5
- **SHARAPOVA** 4-6, 6-2, 6-2
- **WILLIAMS, S.** 6-2, 6-2

Semifinals

- **DAVENPORT** 2-6, 7-6(5), 6-4
- **WILLIAMS, S.** 2-6, 7-5, 8-6

Final

- **SERENA WILLIAMS** 2-6, 6-3, 6-0

Prize Money (US$)	
Winner	$934,050
Runner-up	$466,962
Semifinalists	$233,480
Quarterfinalists	$116,750
Round of 16	$58,381
Round of 32	$35,802
Round of 64	$21,795
Round of 128	$14,015

SERENA WILLIAMS

LLEYTON HEWITT

MARIA SHARAPOVA

LINDSAY DAVENPORT

ROGER FEDERER (l) AND MARAT SAFIN

ANDY RODDICK

RAFAEL NADAL

2005 FRENCH OPEN

MEN'S SINGLES
MAY 23-JUNE 4 • PARIS, FRANCE • CLAY

No.	Player	Nation	First Round
1.	**FEDERER, Roger (1)**	**SUI**	FEDERER
2.	SELA, Dudi (Q)	ISR	6-1, 6-4, 6-0
3.	ALMAGRO, Nicolas	ESP	ALMAGRO
4.	KOHLSCHREIBER, Philipp	GER	7-6(4), 6-4, 6-3
5.	ROCHUS, Christophe	BEL	BEHREND
6.	BEHREND, Tomas (Q)	GER	4-6, 6-2, 7-5, 6-2
7.	LLODRA, Michael	FRA	**GONZALEZ**
8.	**GONZALEZ, Fernando (25)**	**CHI**	7-6(3), 6-3, 6-2
9.	**HRBATY, Dominik (17)**	**SVK**	TIPSAREVIC
10.	TIPSAREVIC, Janko	SCG	6-7(5), 6-3, 3-6, 6-3, 8-6
11.	ARMANDO, Hugo (LL)	USA	VICENTE
12.	VICENTE, Fernando (Q)	ESP	7-6(2), 6-4, 2-6, 4-6, 6-3
13.	VIK, Robin (Q)	CZE	VIK
14.	KIM, Kevin	USA	6-4, 7-6(6), 7-5
15.	MARTIN, Alberto	ESP	**MOYA**
16.	**MOYA, Carlos (14)**	**ESP**	5-7, 6-1, 6-4, 6-2
17.	**NALBANDIAN, David (10)**	**ARG**	**NALBANDIAN**
18.	BAGHDATIS, Marcos	CYP	0-6, 6-4, 6-4, 6-4
19.	BERDYCH, Tomas	CZE	BERDYCH
20.	MORRISON, Jeff	USA	6-3, 6-2, 6-4
21.	HERNANDEZ, Oscar	ESP	HERNANDEZ
22.	GIMENO-TRAVER, Daniel (Q)	ESP	6-7(4), 6-0, 6-3, 6-4
23.	DANIEL, Marcos (Q)	BRA	**ANCIC**
24.	**ANCIC, Mario (18)**	**CRO**	6-2, 6-1, 7-6(4)
25.	**CHELA, Juan Ignacio (31)**	**ARG**	**CHELA**
26.	SCHUETTLER, Rainer	GER	3-6, 6-1, 6-4, 6-3
27.	HANESCU, Victor	ROM	HANESCU
28.	TABARA, Michal	CZE	6-2, 4-6, 6-2, 6-1
29.	HORNA, Luis	PER	HORNA
30.	HAEHNEL, Jerome	FRA	7-6(2), 7-5, 6-3
31.	BRZEZICKI, Juan Pablo (LL)	ARG	**HENMAN**
32.	**HENMAN, Tim (7)**	**GBR**	6-2, 6-1, 6-4
33.	**NADAL, Rafael (4)**	**ESP**	**NADAL**
34.	BURGSMULLER, Lars	GER	6-1, 7-6(4), 6-1
35.	FISH, Mardy	USA	MALISSE
36.	MALISSE, Xavier	BEL	6-2, 6-1, 6-1
37.	WESSELS, Peter	NED	WESSELS
38.	MELLO, Ricardo	BRA	6-4, 6-1, 6-3
39.	BRACCIALI, Daniele (LL)	ITA	**GASQUET**
40.	**GASQUET, Richard (30)**	**FRA**	3-6, 6-3, 6-2, 6-4
41.	**GROSJEAN, Sebastien (23)**	**FRA**	**GROSJEAN**
42.	MONACO, Juan	ARG	7-5, 6-3, 6-1
43.	ASCIONE, Thierry (WC)	FRA	SANGUINETTI
44.	SANGUINETTI, Davide	ITA	3-6, 5-7, 6-0, 6-3, 6-4
45.	PAVEL, Andrei	ROM	SERRA
46.	SERRA, Florent (WC)	FRA	6-2, 6-2, 6-3
47.	SRICHAPHAN, Paradorn	THA	**STEPANEK**
48.	**STEPANEK, Radek (16)**	**CZE**	3-6, 6-3, 6-1, 6-1
49.	**SODERLING, Robin (33)**	**SWE**	**SODERLING**
50.	VERDASCO, Fernando	ESP	1-6, 3-6, 6-3, 6-3, 6-3
51.	LEE, Hyung-Taik	KOR	LEE
52.	CALATRAVA, Alex	ESP	6-4, 2-6, 5-7, 7-6(4), 6-4
53.	SIMON, Gilles (WC)	FRA	PATIENCE
54.	PATIENCE, Olivier (WC)	FRA	6-2, 6-2, 4-6, 6-3
55.	VANEK, Jiri	CZE	**FERRER**
56.	**FERRER, David (20)**	**ESP**	2-6, 7-6(8), 6-4, 6-0
57.	**NOVAK, Jiri (26)**	**CZE**	**NOVAK**
58.	PHAU, Bjorn	GER	4-6, 6-2, 6-3, 6-1
59.	MANTILLA, Felix	ESP	MANTILLA
60.	ZIB, Tomas	CZE	6-2, 6-1, 6-3
61.	TURSUNOV, Dmitry	RUS	TURSUNOV
62.	KOUBEK, Stefan	AUT	4-6, 6-1, 6-4, 6-1
63.	BENNETEAU, Julien	FRA	**GAUDIO**
64.	**GAUDIO, Gaston (5)**	**ARG**	7-5, 6-0, 6-1
65.	**CORIA, Guillermo (8)**	**ARG**	**CORIA**
66.	CARLSEN, Kenneth	DEN	6-4, 6-2, 6-4
67.	DJOKOVIC, Novak (Q)	SCG	DJOKOVIC
68.	GINEPRI, Robby	USA	6-0, 6-0, 6-3
69.	MELZER, Jurgen	AUT	MELZER
70.	ARTHURS, Wayne	AUS	6-4, 6-2, 7-6(4)
71.	MULLER, Gilles	LUX	**YOUZHNY**
72.	**YOUZHNY, Mikhail (29)**	**RUS**	6-4, 6-1, 6-0
73.	**HAAS, Tommy (21)**	**GER**	**HAAS**
74.	MAYER, Floria	GER	6-1, 6-2, 6-4
75.	SPADEA, Vincent	USA	SPADEA
76.	COSTA, Albert	ESP	6-4, 7-6(6), 6-2
77.	GARCIA-LOPEZ, Guillermo	ESP	ROCHUS
78.	ROCHUS, Olivier	BEL	7-6(4), 7-5, 4-6, 6-3
79.	TUKSAR, Sasa (Q)	CRO	**DAVYDENKO**
80.	**DAVYDENKO, Nikolay (12)**	**RUS**	6-2, 6-4, 6-3
81.	**ROBREDO, Tommy (15)**	**ESP**	**ROBREDO**
82.	LUCZAK, Peter (WC)	AUS	4-6, 6-3, 6-3, 6-3
83.	NORMAN, Dick (LL)	BEL	NORMAN
84.	LISNARD, Jean-Rene	FRA	6-1, 6-1, 6-4
85.	KUERTEN, Gustavo	BRA	SANCHEZ
86.	SANCHEZ, David	ESP	6-3, 6-0, 4-6, 6-1
87.	DRAPER, Scott	AUS	**JOHANSSON**
88.	**JOHANSSON, Thomas (19)**	**SWE**	6-7(5), 6-1, 3-6, 6-0, 6-1
89.	**FERRERO, Juan Carlos (32)**	**ESP**	**FERRERO**
90.	BECK, Karol	SVK	6-4, 6-3, 6-3
91.	SANTORO, Fabrice	FRA	HERNYCH
92.	HERNYCH, Jan	CZE	7-6(4), 3-6, 6-1, 4-6, 6-4
93.	ENQVIST, Thomas	SWE	DLOUHY
94.	DLOUHY, Lukas (Q)	CZE	6-2, 7-6(3), 6-1
95.	SLUITER, Raemon	NED	**SAFIN**
96.	**SAFIN, Marat (3)**	**RUS**	6-1, 4-6, 6-4, 6-2
97.	**AGASSI, Andre (6)**	**USA**	NIEMINEN
98.	NIEMINEN, Jarkko (Q)	FIN	7-5, 4-6, 6-7(6), 6-1, 6-0
99.	BJORKMAN, Jonas	SWE	ANDREEV
100.	ANDREEV, Igor	RUS	2-6, 6-2, 6-2, 7-5
101.	CLEMENT, Arnaud (WC)	FRA	CLEMENT
102.	POPP, Alexander	GER	6-2, 6-4, 6-7(1), 6-1
103.	KARLOVIC, Ivo	CRO	**KIEFER**
104.	**KIEFER, Nicolas (28)**	**GER**	6-3, 6-3, 6-4
105.	**LOPEZ, Feliciano (24)**	**ESP**	MATHIEU
106.	MATHIEU, Paul-Henri	FRA	6-2, 6-0, 6-7(5), 6-4
107.	GUCCIONE, Chris (Q)	AUS	GUCCIONE
108.	VENTURA, Santiago	ESP	6-3, 2-6, 6-1, 3-6, 6-2
109.	MONTANES, Albert	ESP	MONTANES
110.	SARGSIAN, Sargis	ARM	6-1, 6-4, 6-0
111.	MONFILS, Gael (WC)	FRA	**CANAS**
112.	**CANAS, Guillermo (9)**	**ARG**	6-3, 6-1, 6-0
113.	**LJUBICIC, Ivan (13)**	**CRO**	PUERTA
114.	PUERTA, Mariano	ARG	7-5, 7-5, 6-2
115.	DUPUIS, Antony (Q)	FRA	VLIEGEN
116.	VLIEGEN, Kristof (Q)	BEL	6-4, 6-1, 6-2
117.	TENCONI, Tomas (Q)	ITA	BLAKE
118.	BLAKE, James (Q)	USA	6-2, 6-4, 7-6(8)
119.	WAWRINKA, Stanislas (Q)	SUI	WAWRINKA
120.	**MASSU, Nicolas (22)**	**CHI**	6-7(4), 6-2, 6-2, 6-4
121.	**VOLANDRI, Filippo (27)**	**ITA**	**VOLANDRI**
122.	SAULNIER, Cyril	FRA	6-0, 6-2, 6-1
123.	RUSEDSKI, Greg	GBR	SARETTA
124.	SARETTA, Flavio (LL)	BRA	6-2, 7-6(7), 6-3
125.	ACASUSO, Jose	ARG	ACASUSO
126.	MIRNYI, Max	BLR	6-4, 7-6(9), 6-2
127.	TSONGA, Jo-Wilfried (WC)	FRA	**RODDICK**
128.	**RODDICK, Andy (2)**	**USA**	6-3, 6-2, 6-4

Second Round

FEDERER 6-3, 7-6(0), 6-2
GONZALEZ 6-3, 6-4, 6-4
VICENTE 6-3, 1-6, 7-6(2), 6-3
MOYA 7-6(6), 6-7(4), 6-3, 6-1
NALBANDIAN 6-3, 6-2, 6-1
ANCIC 4-6, 6-1, 6-2, 6-3
HANESCU 7-5, 6-1, 3-6, 7-5
HORNA 7-5, 6-7(2), 6-3, 6-4
NADAL 6-2, 6-2, 6-4
GASQUET 6-3, 7-6(1), 6-1
GROSJEAN 6-0, 6-3, 6-2
STEPANEK 6-3, 6-4, 6-1
LEE 6-2, 6-3, 6-4
FERRER 6-3, 7-6(5), 7-5
MANTILLA 6-2, 0-6, 3-6, 7-5, 6-3
GAUDIO W/O
CORIA 4-6, 6-2, 3-2 RET.
MELZER 6-3, 6-4, 7-6(5)
HAAS 6-4, 6-3, RET.
DAVYDENKO 3-6, 7-5, 6-2, 6-3
ROBREDO 6-4, 6-2, 6-4
SANCHEZ 6-3, 3-6, 4-6, 7-6(4), 6-4
FERRERO 6-4, 6-4, 6-2
SAFIN 6-7(6), 6-3, 7-5, 6-1
ANDREEV 6-2, 6-4, 6-7(3), 6-2
KIEFER 4-6, 6-2, 6-2, 4-6, 6-4
MATHIEU 6-3, 6-4, 6-4
CANAS 6-1, 6-3, 6-4
PUERTA 6-3, 7-5, 6-2
WAWRINKA 6-7(9), 5-7, 6-1, 6-3, 6-4
VOLANDRI 6-4, 6-1, 6-2
ACASUSO 3-6, 4-6, 6-4, 6-3, 8-6

Third Round

FEDERER 7-6(9), 7-5, 6-2
MOYA 6-4, 7-6(4), 6-7(3), 0-6, 6-4
NALBANDIAN 6-4, 7-6(4), 6-3
HANESCU 6-3, 6-4, 6-4
NADAL 6-4, 6-3, 6-2
GROSJEAN 6-1, 4-6, 3-6, 6-3, 6-4
FERRER 6-3, 6-1, 7-5
GAUDIO 6-4, 6-4, 6-3
CORIA 6-1, 6-1, 7-6(2)
DAVYDENKO 7-5, 6-0, 6-0
ROBREDO 6-4, 6-3, 6-1
SAFIN 7-6(5), 7-5, 1-6, 7-6(2)
KIEFER 6-4, 7-6(7), 3-6, 6-4
CANAS 6-3, 7-6(4), 2-6, 6-7(5), 8-6
PUERTA 1-6, 6-3, 6-1, 6-4
ACASUSO 3-0 RET.

Fourth Round

FEDERER 6-1, 6-4, 6-3
HANESCU 6-3, 4-6, 5-7, 6-1, 6-2
NADAL 6-4, 3-6, 6-0, 6-3
FERRER 2-6, 6-4, 7-6(5), 6-4
DAVYDENKO 2-6, 6-3, 7-6(1), 6-2
ROBREDO 7-5, 1-6, 6-1, 4-6, 8-6
CANAS W/O
PUERTA 6-4, 6-1, 6-1

Quarterfinals

FEDERER 6-2, 7-6(3), 6-3
NADAL 7-5, 6-2, 6-0
DAVYDENKO 3-6, 6-1, 6-2, 4-6, 6-4
PUERTA 6-2, 3-6, 1-6, 6-3, 6-4

Semifinals

NADAL 6-3, 4-6, 6-4, 6-3
PUERTA 6-3, 5-7, 2-6, 6-4, 6-4

Final

RAFAEL NADAL
6-7(6), 6-3, 6-1, 7-5

Prize Money	
Winner	**€880,000**
Runner-up	**€440,000**
Semifinalists	**€200,000**
Quarterfinalists	**€116,180**
Round of 16	**€62,020**
Round of 32	**€36,140**
Round of 64	**€21,795**
Round of 128	**€13,100**

JUSTINE HENIN-HARDENNE

2005 FRENCH OPEN

WOMEN'S SINGLES
MAY 23-JUNE 5 • PARIS, FRANCE • CLAY

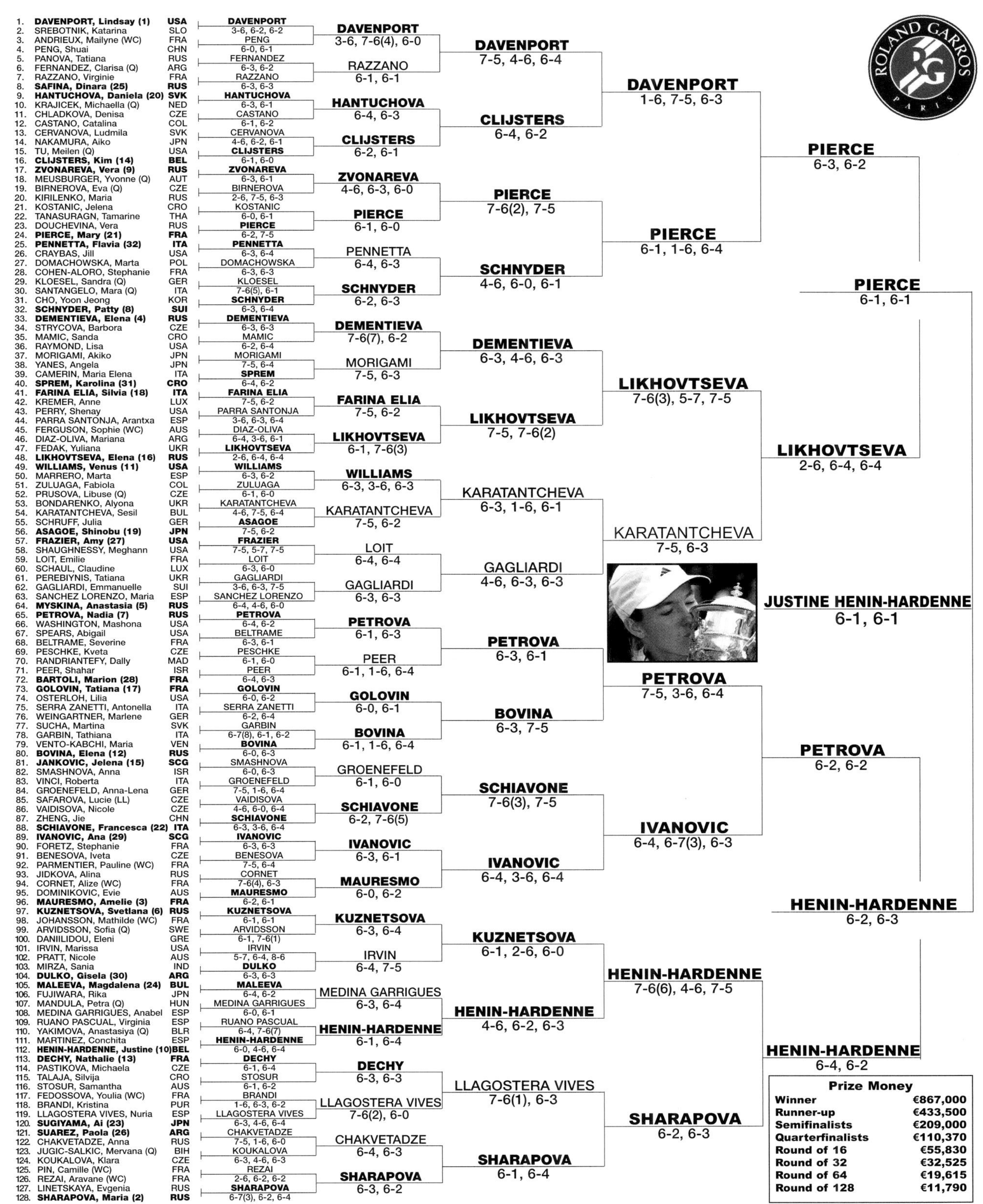

1.	**DAVENPORT, Lindsay (1)**	**USA**
2.	SREBOTNIK, Katarina	SLO
3.	ANDRIEUX, Mailyne (WC)	FRA
4.	PENG, Shuai	CHN
5.	PANOVA, Tatiana	RUS
6.	FERNANDEZ, Clarisa (Q)	ARG
7.	RAZZANO, Virginie	FRA
8.	**SAFINA, Dinara (25)**	**RUS**
9.	**HANTUCHOVA, Daniela (20)**	**SVK**
10.	KRAJICEK, Michaella (Q)	NED
11.	CHLADKOVA, Denisa	CZE
12.	CASTANO, Catalina	COL
13.	CERVANOVA, Ludmila	SVK
14.	NAKAMURA, Aiko	JPN
15.	TU, Meilen (Q)	USA
16.	**CLIJSTERS, Kim (14)**	**BEL**
17.	**ZVONAREVA, Vera (9)**	**RUS**
18.	MEUSBURGER, Yvonne (Q)	AUT
19.	BIRNEROVA, Eva (Q)	CZE
20.	KIRILENKO, Maria	RUS
21.	KOSTANIC, Jelena	CRO
22.	TANASURAGN, Tamarine	THA
23.	DOUCHEVINA, Vera	RUS
24.	**PIERCE, Mary (21)**	**FRA**
25.	**PENNETTA, Flavia (32)**	**ITA**
26.	CRAYBAS, Jill	USA
27.	DOMACHOWSKA, Marta	POL
28.	COHEN-ALORO, Stephanie	FRA
29.	KLOESEL, Sandra (Q)	GER
30.	SANTANGELO, Mara (Q)	ITA
31.	CHO, Yoon Jeong	KOR
32.	**SCHNYDER, Patty (8)**	**SUI**
33.	**DEMENTIEVA, Elena (4)**	**RUS**
34.	STRYCOVA, Barbora	CZE
35.	MAMIC, Sanda	CRO
36.	RAYMOND, Lisa	USA
37.	MORIGAMI, Akiko	JPN
38.	YANES, Angela	JPN
39.	CAMERIN, Maria Elena	ITA
40.	**SPREM, Karolina (31)**	**CRO**
41.	**FARINA ELIA, Silvia (18)**	**ITA**
42.	KREMER, Anne	LUX
43.	PERRY, Shenay	USA
44.	PARRA SANTONJA, Arantxa	ESP
45.	FERGUSON, Sophie (WC)	AUS
46.	DIAZ-OLIVA, Mariana	ARG
47.	FEDAK, Yuliana	UKR
48.	**LIKHOVTSEVA, Elena (16)**	**RUS**
49.	**WILLIAMS, Venus (11)**	**USA**
50.	MARRERO, Marta	ESP
51.	ZULUAGA, Fabiola	COL
52.	PRUSOVA, Libuse (Q)	CZE
53.	BONDARENKO, Alyona	UKR
54.	KARATANTCHEVA, Sesil	BUL
55.	SCHRUFF, Julia	GER
56.	**ASAGOE, Shinobu (19)**	**JPN**
57.	**FRAZIER, Amy (27)**	**USA**
58.	SHAUGHNESSY, Meghann	USA
59.	LOIT, Emilie	FRA
60.	SCHAUL, Claudine	LUX
61.	PEREBIYNIS, Tatiana	UKR
62.	GAGLIARDI, Emmanuelle	SUI
63.	SANCHEZ LORENZO, Maria	ESP
64.	**MYSKINA, Anastasia (5)**	**RUS**
65.	**PETROVA, Nadia (7)**	**RUS**
66.	WASHINGTON, Mashona	USA
67.	SPEARS, Abigail	USA
68.	BELTRAME, Severine	FRA
69.	PESCHKE, Kveta	CZE
70.	RANDRIANTEFY, Dally	MAD
71.	PEER, Shahar	ISR
72.	**BARTOLI, Marion (28)**	**FRA**
73.	**GOLOVIN, Tatiana (17)**	**FRA**
74.	OSTERLOH, Lilia	USA
75.	SERRA ZANETTI, Antonella	ITA
76.	WEINGARTNER, Marlene	GER
77.	SUCHA, Martina	SVK
78.	GARBIN, Tathiana	ITA
79.	VENTO-KABCHI, Maria	VEN
80.	**BOVINA, Elena (12)**	**RUS**
81.	**JANKOVIC, Jelena (15)**	**SCG**
82.	SMASHNOVA, Anna	ISR
83.	VINCI, Roberta	ITA
84.	GROENEFELD, Anna-Lena	GER
85.	SAFAROVA, Lucie (LL)	CZE
86.	VAIDISOVA, Nicole	CZE
87.	ZHENG, Jie	CHN
88.	**SCHIAVONE, Francesca (22)**	**ITA**
89.	**IVANOVIC, Ana (29)**	**SCG**
90.	FORETZ, Stephanie	FRA
91.	BENESOVA, Iveta	CZE
92.	PARMENTIER, Pauline (WC)	FRA
93.	JIDKOVA, Alina	RUS
94.	CORNET, Alize (WC)	FRA
95.	DOMINIKOVIC, Evie	AUS
96.	**MAURESMO, Amelie (3)**	**FRA**
97.	**KUZNETSOVA, Svetlana (6)**	**RUS**
98.	JOHANSSON, Mathilde (WC)	FRA
99.	ARVIDSSON, Sofia (Q)	SWE
100.	DANIILIDOU, Eleni	GRE
101.	IRVIN, Marissa	USA
102.	PRATT, Nicole	AUS
103.	MIRZA, Sania	IND
104.	**DULKO, Gisela (30)**	**ARG**
105.	**MALEEVA, Magdalena (24)**	**BUL**
106.	FUJIWARA, Rika	JPN
107.	MANDULA, Petra (Q)	HUN
108.	MEDINA GARRIGUES, Anabel	ESP
109.	RUANO PASCUAL, Virginia	ESP
110.	YAKIMOVA, Anastasiya (Q)	BLR
111.	MARTINEZ, Conchita	ESP
112.	**HENIN-HARDENNE, Justine (10)**	**BEL**
113.	**DECHY, Nathalie (13)**	**FRA**
114.	PASTIKOVA, Michaela	CZE
115.	TALAJA, Silvija	CRO
116.	STOSUR, Samantha	AUS
117.	FEDOSSOVA, Youlia (WC)	FRA
118.	BRANDI, Kristina	PUR
119.	LLAGOSTERA VIVES, Nuria	ESP
120.	**SUGIYAMA, Ai (23)**	**JPN**
121.	**SUAREZ, Paola (26)**	**ARG**
122.	CHAKVETADZE, Anna	RUS
123.	JUGIC-SALKIC, Mervana (Q)	BIH
124.	KOUKALOVA, Klara	CZE
125.	PIN, Camille (WC)	FRA
126.	REZAI, Aravane (WC)	FRA
127.	LINETSKAYA, Evgenia	RUS
128.	**SHARAPOVA, Maria (2)**	**RUS**

First Round	Second Round	Third Round	Round of 16	Quarterfinals	Semifinals	Final
DAVENPORT 3-6, 6-2, 6-2	**DAVENPORT** 3-6, 7-6(4), 6-0	**DAVENPORT** 7-5, 4-6, 6-4	**DAVENPORT** 1-6, 7-5, 6-3	**PIERCE** 6-3, 6-2	**PIERCE** 6-1, 6-1	**JUSTINE HENIN-HARDENNE** 6-1, 6-1
PENG 6-0, 6-1	RAZZANO 6-1, 6-1	**CLIJSTERS** 6-4, 6-2	**PIERCE** 6-1, 1-6, 6-4	**LIKHOVTSEVA** 2-6, 6-4, 6-4	**HENIN-HARDENNE** 6-2, 6-3	
FERNANDEZ 6-3, 6-2	**HANTUCHOVA** 6-4, 6-3	**PIERCE** 7-6(2), 7-5	**LIKHOVTSEVA** 7-6(3), 5-7, 7-5	**PETROVA** 6-2, 6-2		
RAZZANO 6-3, 6-3	**CLIJSTERS** 6-2, 6-1	**SCHNYDER** 4-6, 6-0, 6-1	KARATANTCHEVA 7-5, 6-3	**HENIN-HARDENNE** 6-4, 6-2		
HANTUCHOVA 6-3, 6-1	**ZVONAREVA** 4-6, 6-3, 6-0	**DEMENTIEVA** 6-3, 4-6, 6-3	**PETROVA** 7-5, 3-6, 6-4			
CASTANO 6-1, 6-2	**PIERCE** 6-1, 6-0	**LIKHOVTSEVA** 7-5, 7-6(2)	**IVANOVIC** 6-4, 6-7(3), 6-3			
CERVANOVA 4-6, 6-2, 6-1	PENNETTA 6-4, 6-3	KARATANTCHEVA 6-3, 1-6, 6-1	**HENIN-HARDENNE** 7-6(6), 4-6, 7-5			
CLIJSTERS 6-1, 6-0	**SCHNYDER** 6-2, 6-3	GAGLIARDI 4-6, 6-3, 6-3	**SHARAPOVA** 6-2, 6-3			
ZVONAREVA 6-3, 6-1	**DEMENTIEVA** 7-6(7), 6-2	**PETROVA** 6-3, 6-1				
BIRNEROVA 2-6, 7-5, 6-3	MORIGAMI 7-5, 6-3	**BOVINA** 6-3, 7-5				
KOSTANIC 6-0, 6-1	**FARINA ELIA** 7-5, 6-2	**SCHIAVONE** 7-6(3), 7-5				
PIERCE 6-2, 7-5	**LIKHOVTSEVA** 6-1, 7-6(3)	**IVANOVIC** 6-4, 3-6, 6-4				
PENNETTA 6-3, 6-4	**WILLIAMS** 6-3, 3-6, 6-3	**KUZNETSOVA** 6-1, 2-6, 6-0				
DOMACHOWSKA 6-3, 6-3	KARATANTCHEVA 7-5, 6-2	**HENIN-HARDENNE** 4-6, 6-2, 6-3				
KLOESEL 7-6(5), 6-1	LOIT 6-4, 6-4	LLAGOSTERA VIVES 7-6(1), 6-3				
SCHNYDER 6-3, 6-4	GAGLIARDI 6-3, 6-3	**SHARAPOVA** 6-1, 6-4				
DEMENTIEVA 6-3, 6-3	**PETROVA** 6-1, 6-3					
MAMIC 6-2, 6-4	PEER 6-1, 1-6, 6-4					
MORIGAMI 7-5, 6-4	**GOLOVIN** 6-0, 6-1					
SPREM 6-4, 6-2	**BOVINA** 6-1, 1-6, 6-4					
FARINA ELIA 7-5, 6-2	GROENEFELD 6-1, 6-0					
PARRA SANTONJA 3-6, 6-3, 6-4	**SCHIAVONE** 6-2, 7-6(5)					
DIAZ-OLIVA 6-4, 3-6, 6-1	**IVANOVIC** 6-3, 6-1					
LIKHOVTSEVA 2-6, 6-4, 6-4	**MAURESMO** 6-0, 6-2					
WILLIAMS 6-3, 6-2	**KUZNETSOVA** 6-3, 6-4					
ZULUAGA 6-1, 6-0	IRVIN 6-4, 7-5					
KARATANTCHEVA 4-6, 7-5, 6-4	MEDINA GARRIGUES 6-3, 6-4					
ASAGOE 7-5, 6-2	**HENIN-HARDENNE** 6-1, 6-4					
FRAZIER 7-5, 5-7, 7-5	**DECHY** 6-3, 6-3					
LOIT 6-3, 6-0	LLAGOSTERA VIVES 7-6(2), 6-0					
GAGLIARDI 3-6, 6-3, 7-5	CHAKVETADZE 6-4, 6-3					
SANCHEZ LORENZO 6-4, 4-6, 6-0	**SHARAPOVA** 6-3, 6-2					
PETROVA 6-4, 6-2						
BELTRAME 6-3, 6-1						
PESCHKE 6-1, 6-0						
PEER 6-4, 6-3						
GOLOVIN 6-0, 6-2						
SERRA ZANETTI 6-2, 6-4						
GARBIN 6-7(8), 6-1, 6-2						
BOVINA 6-0, 6-3						
SMASHNOVA 6-0, 6-3						
GROENEFELD 7-5, 1-6, 6-4						
VAIDISOVA 4-6, 6-0, 6-4						
SCHIAVONE 6-3, 3-6, 6-4						
IVANOVIC 6-3, 6-3						
BENESOVA 7-5, 6-4						
CORNET 7-6(4), 6-3						
MAURESMO 6-2, 6-1						
KUZNETSOVA 6-1, 6-1						
ARVIDSSON 6-1, 7-6(1)						
IRVIN 5-7, 6-4, 8-6						
DULKO 6-3, 6-3						
MALEEVA 6-4, 6-2						
MEDINA GARRIGUES 6-0, 6-1						
RUANO PASCUAL 6-4, 7-6(7)						
HENIN-HARDENNE 6-0, 4-6, 6-4						
DECHY 6-1, 6-4						
STOSUR 6-1, 6-2						
BRANDI 1-6, 6-3, 6-2						
LLAGOSTERA VIVES 6-3, 4-6, 6-4						
CHAKVETADZE 7-5, 1-6, 6-0						
KOUKALOVA 6-3, 4-6, 6-3						
REZAI 2-6, 6-2, 6-2						
SHARAPOVA 6-7(3), 6-2, 6-4						

Prize Money

Winner	**€867,000**
Runner-up	**€433,500**
Semifinalists	**€209,000**
Quarterfinalists	**€110,370**
Round of 16	**€55,830**
Round of 32	**€32,525**
Round of 64	**€19,615**
Round of 128	**€11,790**

MARY PIERCE

RICHARD GASQUET

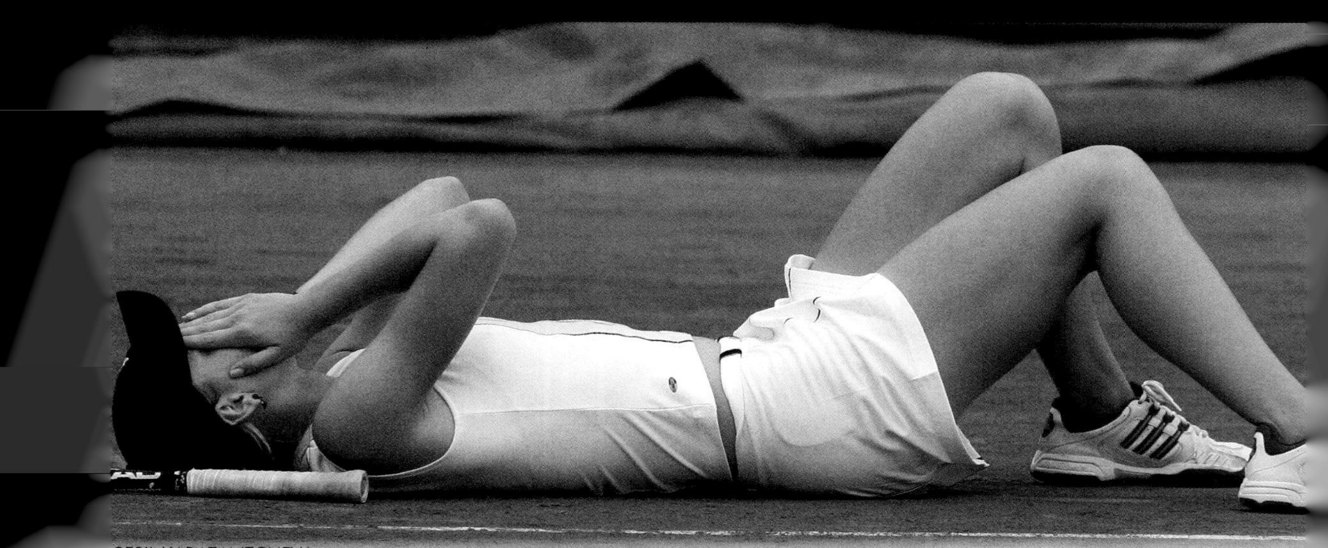

SESIL KARATANTCHEVA

MARIANO PUERTA

YANNICK NOAH

ANA IVANOVIC

ROGER FEDERER (l) AND RAFAEL NADAL (r)

CHRISTIAN BIMES (l) AND MARY PIERCE (r)

MARAT SAFIN

SEBASTIEN GROSJEAN

VENUS WILLIAMS

RAFAEL NADAL

ROGER FEDERER

2005 WIMBLEDON

MEN'S SINGLES
JUNE 20-JULY 3 • LONDON, ENGLAND • GRASS

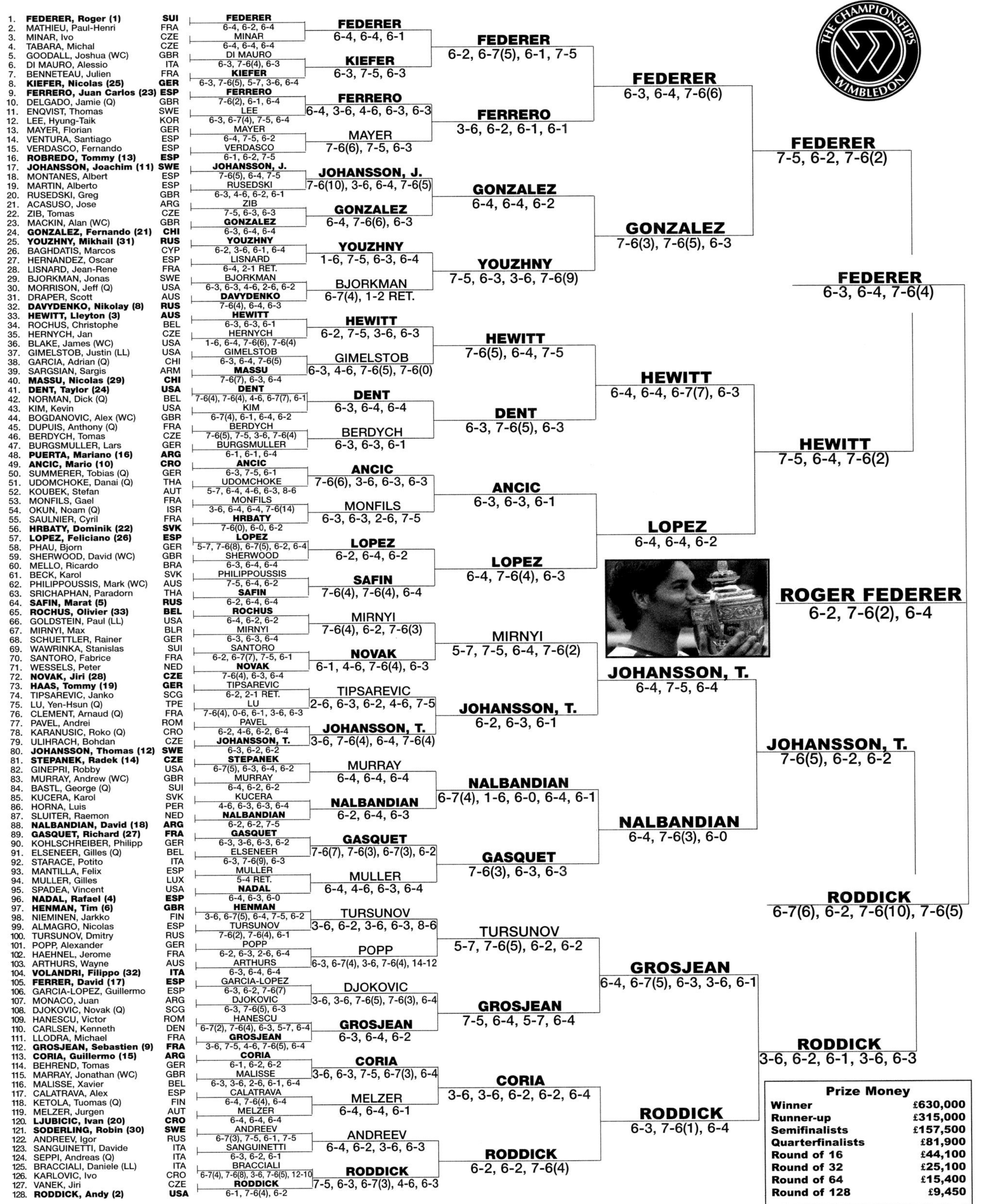

1.	**FEDERER, Roger (1)**	**SUI**
2.	MATHIEU, Paul-Henri	FRA
3.	MINAR, Ivo	CZE
4.	TABARA, Michal	CZE
5.	GOODALL, Joshua (WC)	GBR
6.	DI MAURO, Alessio	ITA
7.	BENNETEAU, Julien	FRA
8.	**KIEFER, Nicolas (25)**	**GER**
9.	**FERRERO, Juan Carlos (23)**	**ESP**
10.	DELGADO, Jamie (Q)	GBR
11.	ENQVIST, Thomas	SWE
12.	LEE, Hyung-Taik	KOR
13.	MAYER, Florian	GER
14.	VENTURA, Santiago	ESP
15.	VERDASCO, Fernando	ESP
16.	**ROBREDO, Tommy (13)**	**ESP**
17.	**JOHANSSON, Joachim (11)**	**SWE**
18.	MONTANES, Albert	ESP
19.	MARTIN, Alberto	ESP
20.	RUSEDSKI, Greg	GBR
21.	ACASUSO, Jose	ARG
22.	ZIB, Tomas	CZE
23.	MACKIN, Alan (WC)	GBR
24.	**GONZALEZ, Fernando (21)**	**CHI**
25.	**YOUZHNY, Mikhail (31)**	**RUS**
26.	BAGHDATIS, Marcos	CYP
27.	HERNANDEZ, Oscar	ESP
28.	LISNARD, Jean-Rene	FRA
29.	BJORKMAN, Jonas	SWE
30.	MORRISON, Jeff (Q)	USA
31.	DRAPER, Scott	AUS
32.	**DAVYDENKO, Nikolay (8)**	**RUS**
33.	**HEWITT, Lleyton (3)**	**AUS**
34.	ROCHUS, Christophe	BEL
35.	HERNYCH, Jan	CZE
36.	BLAKE, James (WC)	USA
37.	GIMELSTOB, Justin (LL)	USA
38.	GARCIA, Adrian (Q)	CHI
39.	SARGSIAN, Sargis	ARM
40.	**MASSU, Nicolas (29)**	**CHI**
41.	**DENT, Taylor (24)**	**USA**
42.	NORMAN, Dick (Q)	BEL
43.	KIM, Kevin	USA
44.	BOGDANOVIC, Alex (WC)	GBR
45.	DUPUIS, Anthony (Q)	FRA
46.	BERDYCH, Tomas	CZE
47.	BURGSMULLER, Lars	GER
48.	**PUERTA, Mariano (16)**	**ARG**
49.	**ANCIC, Mario (10)**	**CRO**
50.	SUMMERER, Tobias (Q)	GER
51.	UDOMCHOKE, Danai (Q)	THA
52.	KOUBEK, Stefan	AUT
53.	MONFILS, Gael	FRA
54.	OKUN, Noam (Q)	ISR
55.	SAULNIER, Cyril	FRA
56.	**HRBATY, Dominik (22)**	**SVK**
57.	**LOPEZ, Feliciano (26)**	**ESP**
58.	PHAU, Bjorn	GER
59.	SHERWOOD, David (WC)	GBR
60.	MELLO, Ricardo	BRA
61.	BECK, Karol	SVK
62.	PHILIPPOUSSIS, Mark (WC)	AUS
63.	SRICHAPHAN, Paradorn	THA
64.	**SAFIN, Marat (5)**	**RUS**
65.	**ROCHUS, Olivier (33)**	**BEL**
66.	GOLDSTEIN, Paul (LL)	USA
67.	MIRNYI, Max	BLR
68.	SCHUETTLER, Rainer	GER
69.	WAWRINKA, Stanislas	SUI
70.	SANTORO, Fabrice	FRA
71.	WESSELS, Peter	NED
72.	**NOVAK, Jiri (28)**	**CZE**
73.	**HAAS, Tommy (19)**	**GER**
74.	TIPSAREVIC, Janko	SCG
75.	LU, Yen-Hsun (Q)	TPE
76.	CLEMENT, Arnaud (Q)	FRA
77.	PAVEL, Andrei	ROM
78.	KARANUSIC, Roko (Q)	CRO
79.	ULIHRACH, Bohdan	CZE
80.	**JOHANSSON, Thomas (12)**	**SWE**
81.	**STEPANEK, Radek (14)**	**CZE**
82.	GINEPRI, Robby	USA
83.	MURRAY, Andrew (WC)	GBR
84.	BASTL, George (Q)	SUI
85.	KUCERA, Karol	SVK
86.	HORNA, Luis	PER
87.	SLUITER, Raemon	NED
88.	**NALBANDIAN, David (18)**	**ARG**
89.	**GASQUET, Richard (27)**	**FRA**
90.	KOHLSCHREIBER, Philipp	GER
91.	ELSENEER, Gilles (Q)	BEL
92.	STARACE, Potito	ITA
93.	MANTILLA, Felix	ESP
94.	MULLER, Gilles	LUX
95.	SPADEA, Vincent	USA
96.	**NADAL, Rafael (4)**	**ESP**
97.	**HENMAN, Tim (6)**	**GBR**
98.	NIEMINEN, Jarkko	FIN
99.	ALMAGRO, Nicolas	ESP
100.	TURSUNOV, Dmitry	RUS
101.	POPP, Alexander	GER
102.	HAEHNEL, Jerome	FRA
103.	ARTHURS, Wayne	AUS
104.	**VOLANDRI, Filippo (32)**	**ITA**
105.	**FERRER, David (17)**	**ESP**
106.	GARCIA-LOPEZ, Guillermo	ESP
107.	MONACO, Juan	ARG
108.	DJOKOVIC, Novak (Q)	SCG
109.	HANESCU, Victor	ROM
110.	CARLSEN, Kenneth	DEN
111.	LLODRA, Michael	FRA
112.	**GROSJEAN, Sebastien (9)**	**FRA**
113.	**CORIA, Guillermo (15)**	**ARG**
114.	BEHREND, Tomas	GER
115.	MARRAY, Jonathan (WC)	GBR
116.	MALISSE, Xavier	BEL
117.	CALATRAVA, Alex	ESP
118.	KETOLA, Tuomas (Q)	FIN
119.	MELZER, Jurgen	AUT
120.	**LJUBICIC, Ivan (20)**	**CRO**
121.	**SODERLING, Robin (30)**	**SWE**
122.	ANDREEV, Igor	RUS
123.	SANGUINETTI, Davide	ITA
124.	SEPPI, Andreas (Q)	ITA
125.	BRACCIALI, Daniele (LL)	ITA
126.	KARLOVIC, Ivo	CRO
127.	VANEK, Jiri	CZE
128.	**RODDICK, Andy (2)**	**USA**

First Round Winner	Score
FEDERER	6-4, 6-2, 6-4
MINAR	6-4, 6-4, 6-4
DI MAURO	6-3, 7-6(4), 6-3
KIEFER	6-3, 7-6(5), 5-7, 3-6, 6-4
FERRERO	7-6(2), 6-1, 6-4
LEE	6-3, 6-7(4), 7-5, 6-4
MAYER	6-4, 7-5, 6-2
VERDASCO	6-1, 6-2, 7-5
JOHANSSON, J.	7-6(5), 6-4, 7-5
RUSEDSKI	6-3, 4-6, 6-2, 6-1
ZIB	7-5, 6-3, 6-3
GONZALEZ	6-3, 6-4, 6-4
YOUZHNY	6-2, 3-6, 6-1, 6-4
LISNARD	6-4, 2-1 RET.
BJORKMAN	6-3, 6-3, 4-6, 2-6, 6-2
DAVYDENKO	7-6(4), 6-4, 6-3
HEWITT	6-3, 6-3, 6-1
HERNYCH	1-6, 6-4, 7-6(6), 7-6(4)
GIMELSTOB	6-3, 6-4, 7-6(5)
MASSU	7-6(7), 6-3, 6-4
DENT	7-6(4), 7-6(4), 4-6, 6-7(7), 6-1
KIM	6-7(4), 6-1, 6-4, 6-2
BERDYCH	7-6(5), 7-5, 3-6, 7-6(4)
BURGSMULLER	6-1, 6-1, 6-4
ANCIC	6-3, 7-5, 6-1
UDOMCHOKE	5-7, 6-4, 4-6, 6-3, 8-6
MONFILS	3-6, 6-4, 6-4, 7-6(14)
HRBATY	7-6(0), 6-0, 6-2
LOPEZ	5-7, 7-6(8), 6-7(5), 6-2, 6-4
SHERWOOD	6-3, 6-4, 6-4
PHILIPPOUSSIS	7-5, 6-4, 6-2
SAFIN	6-2, 6-4, 6-4
ROCHUS	6-4, 6-2, 6-2
MIRNYI	6-3, 6-3, 6-4
SANTORO	6-2, 6-7(7), 7-5, 6-1
NOVAK	7-6(4), 6-3, 6-4
TIPSAREVIC	6-2, 2-1 RET.
LU	7-6(4), 0-6, 6-1, 3-6, 6-3
PAVEL	6-2, 4-6, 6-2, 6-4
JOHANSSON, T.	6-3, 6-2, 6-2
STEPANEK	6-7(5), 6-3, 6-4, 6-2
MURRAY	6-4, 6-2, 6-2
KUCERA	4-6, 6-3, 6-3, 6-4
NALBANDIAN	6-2, 6-2, 7-5
GASQUET	6-3, 3-6, 6-3, 6-2
ELSENEER	6-3, 7-6(9), 6-3
MULLER	5-4 RET.
NADAL	6-4, 6-3, 6-0
HENMAN	3-6, 6-7(5), 6-4, 7-5, 6-2
TURSUNOV	7-6(2), 7-6(4), 6-1
POPP	6-2, 6-3, 2-6, 6-4
ARTHURS	6-3, 6-4, 6-4
GARCIA-LOPEZ	6-3, 6-2, 7-6(7)
DJOKOVIC	6-3, 7-6(5), 6-3
HANESCU	6-7(2), 7-6(4), 6-3, 5-7, 6-4
GROSJEAN	3-6, 7-5, 4-6, 7-6(5), 6-4
CORIA	6-1, 6-2, 6-2
MALISSE	6-3, 3-6, 2-6, 6-1, 6-4
CALATRAVA	6-4, 7-6(4), 6-4
MELZER	6-4, 6-4, 6-4
ANDREEV	6-7(3), 7-5, 6-1, 7-5
SANGUINETTI	6-3, 6-2, 6-1
BRACCIALI	6-7(4), 7-6(8), 3-6, 7-6(5), 12-10
RODDICK	6-1, 7-6(4), 6-2

Second Round Winner	Score
FEDERER	6-4, 6-4, 6-1
KIEFER	6-3, 7-5, 6-3
FERRERO	6-4, 3-6, 4-6, 6-3, 6-3
MAYER	7-6(6), 7-5, 6-3
JOHANSSON, J.	7-6(10), 3-6, 6-4, 7-6(5)
GONZALEZ	6-4, 7-6(6), 6-3
YOUZHNY	1-6, 7-5, 6-3, 6-4
BJORKMAN	6-7(4), 1-2 RET.
HEWITT	6-2, 7-5, 3-6, 6-3
GIMELSTOB	6-3, 4-6, 7-6(5), 7-6(0)
DENT	6-3, 6-4, 6-4
BERDYCH	6-3, 6-3, 6-1
ANCIC	7-6(6), 3-6, 6-3, 6-3
MONFILS	6-3, 6-3, 2-6, 7-5
LOPEZ	6-2, 6-4, 6-2
SAFIN	7-6(4), 7-6(4), 6-4
MIRNYI	7-6(4), 6-2, 7-6(3)
NOVAK	6-1, 4-6, 7-6(4), 6-3
TIPSAREVIC	2-6, 6-3, 6-2, 4-6, 7-5
JOHANSSON, T.	3-6, 7-6(4), 6-4, 7-6(4)
MURRAY	6-4, 6-4, 6-4
NALBANDIAN	6-2, 6-4, 6-3
GASQUET	7-6(7), 7-6(3), 6-7(3), 6-2
MULLER	6-4, 4-6, 6-3, 6-4
TURSUNOV	3-6, 6-2, 3-6, 6-3, 8-6
POPP	6-3, 6-7(4), 3-6, 7-6(4), 14-12
DJOKOVIC	3-6, 3-6, 7-6(5), 7-6(3), 6-4
GROSJEAN	6-3, 6-4, 6-2
CORIA	3-6, 6-3, 7-5, 6-7(3), 6-4
MELZER	6-4, 6-4, 6-1
ANDREEV	6-4, 6-2, 3-6, 6-3
RODDICK	7-5, 6-3, 6-7(3), 4-6, 6-3

Third Round Winner	Score
FEDERER	6-2, 6-7(5), 6-1, 7-5
FERRERO	3-6, 6-2, 6-1, 6-1
GONZALEZ	6-4, 6-4, 6-2
YOUZHNY	7-5, 6-3, 3-6, 7-6(9)
HEWITT	7-6(5), 6-4, 7-5
DENT	6-3, 7-6(5), 6-3
ANCIC	6-3, 6-3, 6-1
LOPEZ	6-4, 7-6(4), 6-3
MIRNYI	5-7, 7-5, 6-4, 7-6(2)
JOHANSSON, T.	6-2, 6-3, 6-1
NALBANDIAN	6-7(4), 1-6, 6-0, 6-4, 6-1
GASQUET	7-6(3), 6-3, 6-3
TURSUNOV	5-7, 7-6(5), 6-2, 6-2
GROSJEAN	7-5, 6-4, 5-7, 6-4
CORIA	3-6, 3-6, 6-2, 6-2, 6-4
RODDICK	6-2, 6-2, 7-6(4)

Fourth Round Winner	Score
FEDERER	6-3, 6-4, 7-6(6)
GONZALEZ	7-6(3), 7-6(5), 6-3
HEWITT	6-4, 6-4, 6-7(7), 6-3
LOPEZ	6-4, 6-4, 6-2
JOHANSSON, T.	6-4, 7-5, 6-4
NALBANDIAN	6-4, 7-6(3), 6-0
GROSJEAN	6-4, 6-7(5), 6-3, 3-6, 6-1
RODDICK	6-3, 7-6(1), 6-4

Quarterfinal Winner	Score
FEDERER	7-5, 6-2, 7-6(2)
HEWITT	7-5, 6-4, 7-6(2)
JOHANSSON, T.	7-6(5), 6-2, 6-2
RODDICK	3-6, 6-2, 6-1, 3-6, 6-3

Semifinal Winner	Score
FEDERER	6-3, 6-4, 7-6(4)
RODDICK	6-7(6), 6-2, 7-6(10), 7-6(5)

ROGER FEDERER
6-2, 7-6(2), 6-4

Prize Money	
Winner	**£630,000**
Runner-up	**£315,000**
Semifinalists	**£157,500**
Quarterfinalists	**£81,900**
Round of 16	**£44,100**
Round of 32	**£25,100**
Round of 64	**£15,400**
Round of 128	**£9,450**

VENUS WILLIAMS

2005 WIMBLEDON

WOMEN'S SINGLES
JUNE 20-JULY 3 • LONDON, ENGLAND • GRASS

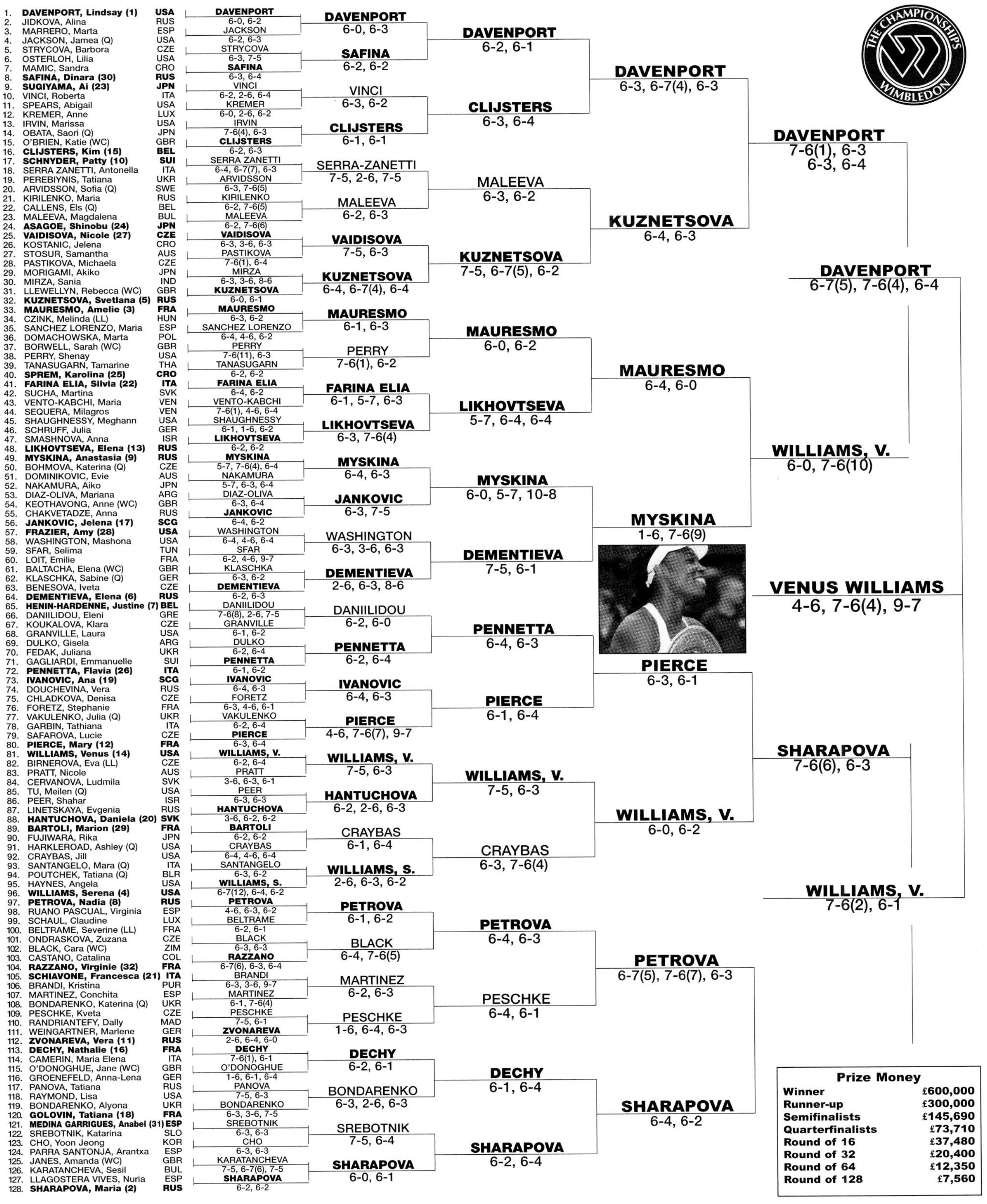

First Round and Second Round

No.	Player	Country	Second-round entrant / score
1.	**DAVENPORT, Lindsay (1)**	**USA**	**DAVENPORT**
2.	JIDKOVA, Alina	RUS	6-0, 6-2
3.	MARRERO, Marta	ESP	JACKSON
4.	JACKSON, Jamea (Q)	USA	6-2, 6-3
5.	STRYCOVA, Barbora	CZE	STRYCOVA
6.	OSTERLOH, Lilia	USA	6-3, 7-5
7.	MAMIC, Sandra	CRO	**SAFINA**
8.	**SAFINA, Dinara (30)**	**RUS**	6-3, 6-4
9.	**SUGIYAMA, Ai (23)**	**JPN**	VINCI
10.	VINCI, Roberta	ITA	6-2, 2-6, 6-4
11.	SPEARS, Abigail	USA	KREMER
12.	KREMER, Anne	LUX	6-0, 2-6, 6-2
13.	IRVIN, Marissa	USA	IRVIN
14.	OBATA, Saori (Q)	JPN	7-6(4), 6-3
15.	O'BRIEN, Katie (WC)	GBR	**CLIJSTERS**
16.	**CLIJSTERS, Kim (15)**	**BEL**	6-2, 6-3
17.	**SCHNYDER, Patty (10)**	**SUI**	SERRA ZANETTI
18.	SERRA ZANETTI, Antonella	ITA	6-4, 6-7(7), 6-3
19.	PEREBIYNIS, Tatiana	UKR	ARVIDSSON
20.	ARVIDSSON, Sofia (Q)	SWE	6-3, 7-6(5)
21.	KIRILENKO, Maria	RUS	KIRILENKO
22.	CALLENS, Els (Q)	BEL	6-2, 7-6(5)
23.	MALEEVA, Magdalena	BUL	MALEEVA
24.	**ASAGOE, Shinobu (24)**	**JPN**	6-2, 7-6(6)
25.	**VAIDISOVA, Nicole (27)**	**CZE**	**VAIDISOVA**
26.	KOSTANIC, Jelena	CRO	6-3, 3-6, 6-3
27.	STOSUR, Samantha	AUS	PASTIKOVA
28.	PASTIKOVA, Michaela	CZE	7-6(1), 6-4
29.	MORIGAMI, Akiko	JPN	MIRZA
30.	MIRZA, Sania	IND	6-3, 3-6, 8-6
31.	LLEWELLYN, Rebecca (WC)	GBR	**KUZNETSOVA**
32.	**KUZNETSOVA, Svetlana (5)**	**RUS**	6-0, 6-1
33.	**MAURESMO, Amelie (3)**	**FRA**	**MAURESMO**
34.	CZINK, Melinda (LL)	HUN	6-3, 6-2
35.	SANCHEZ LORENZO, Maria	ESP	SANCHEZ LORENZO
36.	DOMACHOWSKA, Marta	POL	6-4, 4-6, 6-2
37.	BORWELL, Sarah (WC)	GBR	PERRY
38.	PERRY, Shenay	USA	7-6(11), 6-3
39.	TANASUGARN, Tamarine	THA	TANASUGARN
40.	**SPREM, Karolina (25)**	**CRO**	6-2, 6-2
41.	**FARINA ELIA, Silvia (22)**	**ITA**	**FARINA ELIA**
42.	SUCHA, Martina	SVK	6-4, 6-2
43.	VENTO-KABCHI, Maria	VEN	VENTO-KABCHI
44.	SEQUERA, Milagros	VEN	7-6(1), 4-6, 6-4
45.	SHAUGHNESSY, Meghann	USA	SHAUGHNESSY
46.	SCHRUFF, Julia	GER	6-1, 1-6, 6-2
47.	SMASHNOVA, Anna	ISR	**LIKHOVTSEVA**
48.	**LIKHOVTSEVA, Elena (13)**	**RUS**	6-2, 6-2
49.	**MYSKINA, Anastasia (9)**	**RUS**	**MYSKINA**
50.	BOHMOVA, Katerina (Q)	CZE	5-7, 7-6(4), 6-4
51.	DOMINIKOVIC, Evie	AUS	NAKAMURA
52.	NAKAMURA, Aiko	JPN	5-7, 6-3, 6-4
53.	DIAZ-OLIVA, Mariana	ARG	DIAZ-OLIVA
54.	KEOTHAVONG, Anne (WC)	GBR	6-3, 6-4
55.	CHAKVETADZE, Anna	RUS	**JANKOVIC**
56.	**JANKOVIC, Jelena (17)**	**SCG**	6-4, 6-2
57.	**FRAZIER, Amy (28)**	**USA**	WASHINGTON
58.	WASHINGTON, Mashona	USA	6-4, 4-6, 6-4
59.	SFAR, Selima	TUN	SFAR
60.	LOIT, Emilie	FRA	6-2, 4-6, 9-7
61.	BALTACHA, Elena (WC)	GBR	KLASCHKA
62.	KLASCHKA, Sabine (Q)	GER	6-3, 6-2
63.	BENESOVA, Iveta	CZE	**DEMENTIEVA**
64.	**DEMENTIEVA, Elena (6)**	**RUS**	6-2, 6-3
65.	**HENIN-HARDENNE, Justine (7)**	**BEL**	DANIILIDOU
66.	DANIILIDOU, Eleni	GRE	7-6(8), 2-6, 7-5
67.	KOUKALOVA, Klara	CZE	GRANVILLE
68.	GRANVILLE, Laura	USA	6-1, 6-2
69.	DULKO, Gisela	ARG	DULKO
70.	FEDAK, Juliana	UKR	6-2, 6-4
71.	GAGLIARDI, Emmanuelle	SUI	**PENNETTA**
72.	**PENNETTA, Flavia (26)**	**ITA**	6-1, 6-2
73.	**IVANOVIC, Ana (19)**	**SCG**	**IVANOVIC**
74.	DOUCHEVINA, Vera	RUS	6-4, 6-3
75.	CHLADKOVA, Denisa	CZE	FORETZ
76.	FORETZ, Stephanie	FRA	6-3, 4-6, 6-1
77.	VAKULENKO, Julia (Q)	UKR	VAKULENKO
78.	GARBIN, Tathiana	ITA	6-2, 6-4
79.	SAFAROVA, Lucie	CZE	**PIERCE**
80.	**PIERCE, Mary (12)**	**FRA**	6-3, 6-4
81.	**WILLIAMS, Venus (14)**	**USA**	**WILLIAMS, V.**
82.	BIRNEROVA, Eva (LL)	CZE	6-2, 6-4
83.	PRATT, Nicole	AUS	PRATT
84.	CERVANOVA, Ludmila	SVK	3-6, 6-3, 6-1
85.	TU, Meilen (Q)	USA	PEER
86.	PEER, Shahar	ISR	6-3, 6-3
87.	LINETSKAYA, Evgenia	RUS	**HANTUCHOVA**
88.	**HANTUCHOVA, Daniela (20)**	**SVK**	3-6, 6-2, 6-2
89.	**BARTOLI, Marion (29)**	**FRA**	**BARTOLI**
90.	FUJIWARA, Rika	JPN	6-2, 6-2
91.	HARKLEROAD, Ashley (Q)	USA	CRAYBAS
92.	CRAYBAS, Jill	USA	6-4, 4-6, 6-4
93.	SANTANGELO, Mara (Q)	ITA	SANTANGELO
94.	POUTCHEK, Tatiana (Q)	BLR	6-3, 6-2
95.	HAYNES, Angela	USA	**WILLIAMS, S.**
96.	**WILLIAMS, Serena (4)**	**USA**	6-7(12), 6-4, 6-2
97.	**PETROVA, Nadia (8)**	**RUS**	**PETROVA**
98.	RUANO PASCUAL, Virginia	ESP	4-6, 6-3, 6-2
99.	SCHAUL, Claudine	LUX	BELTRAME
100.	BELTRAME, Severine (LL)	FRA	6-2, 6-1
101.	ONDRASKOVA, Zuzana	CZE	BLACK
102.	BLACK, Cara (WC)	ZIM	6-3, 6-3
103.	CASTANO, Catalina	COL	**RAZZANO**
104.	**RAZZANO, Virginie (32)**	**FRA**	6-7(6), 6-3, 6-4
105.	**SCHIAVONE, Francesca (21)**	**ITA**	BRANDI
106.	BRANDI, Kristina	PUR	6-3, 3-6, 9-7
107.	MARTINEZ, Conchita	ESP	MARTINEZ
108.	BONDARENKO, Katerina (Q)	UKR	6-1, 7-6(4)
109.	PESCHKE, Kveta	CZE	PESCHKE
110.	RANDRIANTEFY, Dally	MAD	7-5, 6-1
111.	WEINGARTNER, Marlene	GER	**ZVONAREVA**
112.	**ZVONAREVA, Vera (11)**	**RUS**	2-6, 6-4, 6-0
113.	**DECHY, Nathalie (16)**	**FRA**	**DECHY**
114.	CAMERIN, Maria Elena	ITA	7-6(1), 6-1
115.	O'DONOGHUE, Jane (WC)	GBR	O'DONOGHUE
116.	GROENEFELD, Anna-Lena	GER	1-6, 6-1, 6-4
117.	PANOVA, Tatiana	RUS	PANOVA
118.	RAYMOND, Lisa	USA	7-5, 6-3
119.	BONDARENKO, Alyona	UKR	BONDARENKO
120.	**GOLOVIN, Tatiana (18)**	**FRA**	6-3, 3-6, 7-5
121.	**MEDINA GARRIGUES, Anabel (31)**	**ESP**	SREBOTNIK
122.	SREBOTNIK, Katarina	SLO	6-3, 6-3
123.	CHO, Yoon Jeong	KOR	CHO
124.	PARRA SANTONJA, Arantxa	ESP	6-3, 6-3
125.	JANES, Amanda (WC)	GBR	KARATANCHEVA
126.	KARATANCHEVA, Sesil	BUL	7-5, 6-7(6), 7-5
127.	LLAGOSTERA VIVES, Nuria	ESP	**SHARAPOVA**
128.	**SHARAPOVA, Maria (2)**	**RUS**	6-2, 6-2

Third Round

DAVENPORT 6-0, 6-3
SAFINA 6-2, 6-2
VINCI 6-3, 6-2
CLIJSTERS 6-1, 6-1
SERRA-ZANETTI 7-5, 2-6, 7-5
MALEEVA 6-2, 6-3
VAIDISOVA 7-5, 6-3
KUZNETSOVA 6-4, 6-7(4), 6-4
MAURESMO 6-1, 6-3
PERRY 7-6(1), 6-2
FARINA ELIA 6-1, 5-7, 6-3
LIKHOVTSEVA 6-3, 7-6(4)
MYSKINA 6-4, 6-3
JANKOVIC 6-3, 7-5
WASHINGTON 6-3, 3-6, 6-3
DEMENTIEVA 2-6, 6-3, 8-6
DANIILIDOU 6-2, 6-0
PENNETTA 6-2, 6-4
IVANOVIC 6-4, 6-3
PIERCE 4-6, 7-6(7), 9-7
WILLIAMS, V. 7-5, 6-3
HANTUCHOVA 6-2, 2-6, 6-3
CRAYBAS 6-1, 6-4
WILLIAMS, S. 2-6, 6-3, 6-2
PETROVA 6-1, 6-2
BLACK 6-4, 7-6(5)
MARTINEZ 6-2, 6-3
PESCHKE 1-6, 6-4, 6-3
DECHY 6-2, 6-1
BONDARENKO 6-3, 2-6, 6-3
SREBOTNIK 7-5, 6-4
SHARAPOVA 6-0, 6-1

Round of 16

DAVENPORT 6-2, 6-1
CLIJSTERS 6-3, 6-4
MALEEVA 6-3, 6-2
KUZNETSOVA 7-5, 6-7(5), 6-2
MAURESMO 6-0, 6-2
LIKHOVTSEVA 5-7, 6-4, 6-4
MYSKINA 6-0, 5-7, 10-8
DEMENTIEVA 7-5, 6-1
PENNETTA 6-4, 6-3
PIERCE 6-1, 6-4
WILLIAMS, V. 7-5, 6-3
CRAYBAS 6-3, 7-6(4)
PETROVA 6-4, 6-3
PESCHKE 6-4, 6-1
DECHY 6-1, 6-4
SHARAPOVA 6-2, 6-4

Quarterfinals

DAVENPORT 6-3, 6-7(4), 6-3
KUZNETSOVA 6-4, 6-3
MAURESMO 6-4, 6-0
MYSKINA 1-6, 7-6(9)
PIERCE 6-3, 6-1
WILLIAMS, V. 6-0, 6-2
PETROVA 6-7(5), 7-6(7), 6-3
SHARAPOVA 6-4, 6-2

Semifinals

DAVENPORT 7-6(1), 6-3
6-3, 6-4
WILLIAMS, V. 6-0, 7-6(10)
SHARAPOVA 7-6(6), 6-3
WILLIAMS, V. 7-6(2), 6-1

Final

DAVENPORT 6-7(5), 7-6(4), 6-4

VENUS WILLIAMS
4-6, 7-6(4), 9-7

Prize Money

Winner	**£600,000**
Runner-up	**£300,000**
Semifinalists	**£145,690**
Quarterfinalists	**£73,710**
Round of 16	**£37,480**
Round of 32	**£20,400**
Round of 64	**£12,350**
Round of 128	**£7,560**

MARIA SHARAPOVA

LLEYTON HEWITT (front) AND ROGER FEDERER

ANGELA HAYNES

JILL CRAYBAS (l) AND VENUS WILLIAMS(r)

NDY RODDICK

BOB BRYAN (l) AND MIKE BRYAN (r)

(l-r) GUILLERMO VILAS, ILIE NASTASE, MANSOUR BAHRAMI AND GENE MAYER

WESLEY MOODIE (l) AND STEPHEN HUSS (r)

ANDREW MURRAY

THOMAS JOHANSSON

SERENA WILLIAMS

INDSAY DAVENPORT (l) AND KIM CLIJSTERS (r)

AMELIE MAURESMO

DAVID NALBANDIAN

TAYLOR DENT

PHOTOGRAPHER CREDITS

cover	Susan Mullane
back cover	Ed Goldman
Page 1	Ron Angle
Page 2-3	Evan Pinkus
Page 4-5	Susan Mullane
Page 6-7	Art Seitz
Page 8	Ron Angle
Page 10	Ron Angle
Page 12-13	Ron Angle
Page 14-15	Paul Zimmer
Page 16-17	Ron Angle
Page 18-19	Evans Pinkus
Page 20-21	Paul Zimmer
Page 22-25	Ron Angle
Page 26-29	Paul Zimmer
Page 30	Michael Cole
Page 32-33	Ron Angle
Page 34	Michael Cole
Page 36-37	Susan Mullane
Page 38-39	Michael Cole
Page 41-42	Ron Angle
Page 44-45	Paul Zimmer
Page 46-47	Ron Angle
Page 48-49	Paul Zimmer
Page 50-52	Ron Angle
Page 53	Melchior DiGiacomo
Page 54-56	Ron Angle
Page 57	Evans Pinkus
Page 58-59	Paul Zimmer
Page 60	Ron Angle
Page 61	Paul Zimmer
Page 62	Cynthia Lum
Page 63	Susan Mullane
Page 64	Fred Mullane
Page 66-67	Ron Angle
Page 68-69	Paul Zimmer
Page 70	Susan Mullane
Page 71	Bob Straus
Page 73	Fred Mullane
Page 74-75	Ron Angle
Page 76-79	Paul Zimmer
Page 80	Evan Pinkus
Page 82-83	Michael Cole
Page 84	Susan Mullane
Page 85	Fred Mullane
Page 86-87	Paul Zimmer
Page 88-89	Evan Pinkus
Page 91	Ron Angle
Page 92-93	Paul Zimmer
Page 94-96	Susan Mullane
Page 97-99	Ron Angle
Page 100	Susan Mullane
Page 101-103	Paul Zimmer
Page 104-105	Ron Angle
Page 106	Michael Cole
Page 107	Ron Angle
Page 108	Michael Cole
Page 109-117	Paul Zimmer
Page 118-119	Ron Angle
Page 120-125	Paul Zimmer
Page 126	Ron Angle
Page 127	Paul Zimmer
Page 128-131	Susan Mullane
Page 132	Art Seitz
Page 136-138	Paul Zimmer
Page 139-140	Ron Angle
Page 141	Michael Baz
Page 142	Ron Angle
Page 143	Michael Baz
Page 144	Paul Zimmer
Page 145	Susan Mullane
Page 146	Paul Zimmer
Page 147-148	Susan Mullane
Page 149	clockwise: Paul Zimmer Art Seitz Michael Cole
Page 150	Paul Zimmer
Page 151	clockwise: Susan Mullane Ron Angle Ron Angle Michael Cole
Page 152	Paul Zimmer
Page 153	Susan Mullane
Page 154	Paul Zimmer
Page 155	Ron Angle
Page 156	clockwise: Ron Angle Art Seitz Angelo Tonelli Ron Angle
Page 157	clockwise: Susan Mullane Paul Zimmer Art Seitz
Page 158	clockwise: Paul Zimmer Fred Mullane Susan Mullane Paul Zimmer
Page 159	clockwise: Paul Zimmer Paul Zimmer Paul Zimmer Michael Cole